Charles Sumner

Speech of Hon. Charles Sumner on the Cession of Russian America to the United States

Charles Sumner

Speech of Hon. Charles Sumner on the Cession of Russian America to the United States

ISBN/EAN: 9783337169169

Printed in Europe, USA, Canada, Australia, Japan

Cover: Foto ©ninafisch / pixelio.de

More available books at **www.hansebooks.com**

SPEECH

OF

HON. CHARLES SUMNER,

OF MASSACHUSETTS,

ON

THE CESSION OF RUSSIAN AMERICA

TO

THE UNITED STATES.

Thirteen governments founded on the natural authority of the people alone, without a pretense of miracle or mystery, and *which are destined to spread over the northern part of that whole quarter of the globe,* are a great point gained in favor of the rights of mankind.—*John Adams's Preface to his Defense of American Constitutions, dated at Grosvenor Square, London, January* 1, 1787.

WASHINGTON:
PRINTED AT THE CONGRESSIONAL GLOBE OFFICE.
1867.

SPEECH.

Mr. PRESIDENT: You have just listened to the reading of the treaty by which Russia cedes to the United States all her possessions on the North American continent in consideration of $7,200,000, to be paid by the United States. On the one side is the cession of a vast country with its jurisdiction and its resources of all kinds: on the other side is the purchase-money. Such is this transaction on its face.

BOUNDARIES AND CONFIGURATION.

In endeavoring to estimate its character I am glad to begin with what is clear and beyond question. I refer to the boundaries fixed by the treaty. Commencing at the parallel of 54° 40' north latitude, so famous in our history, the line ascends Portland channel to the mountains, which it follows on their summits to the point of intersection with the 141° west longitude, which line it ascends to the Frozen ocean, or, if you please, to the north pole. This is the eastern boundary, separating this region from the British possessions, and it is borrowed from the treaty between Russia and Great Britain in 1825, establishing the relations between these two Powers on this continent. It will be seen that this boundary is old; the rest is new. Starting from the Frozen ocean the western boundary descends Behring straits, midway between the two islands of Krusenstern and Ratmanov, to the parallel of 65° 30', just below where the continents of America and Asia approach each other the nearest; and from this point it proceeds in a course nearly southwest through Behring straits, midway between the island of St. Lawrence and Cape Chonkotski, to the meridian of 172° west longitude, and thence, in a southwesterly direction, traversing Behring sea, midway between the island of Attou on the east and Copper island on the west, to the meridian of 193° west longitude, leaving the prolonged group of the Aleutian islands in the possessions now transferred to the United States, and making the western boundary of our country the dividing line which separates Asia from America.

Look at the map and see the configuration of this extensive region, whose estimated area is more than five hundred and seventy thousand square miles. I speak by the authority of our own coast survey. Including the Sitkan archipelago at the south, it takes a margin of the main land, fronting on the ocean thirty miles broad and three hundred miles long, to Mount St. Elias, the highest peak of the continent, when it turns with an elbow to the west, and then along Behring straits northerly, when it rounds to the east along the Frozen ocean. Here are upwards of four thousand statute miles of coast, indented by capacious bays and commodious harbors without number, embracing the peninsula of Alaska, one of the most remarkable in the world, fifty miles in breadth and three hundred miles in length; piled with mountains, many volcanic and some still smoking; penetrated by navigable rivers, one of which is among the largest of the world; studded with islands which stand like sentinels on the coast, and flanked by that narrow Aleutian range which, starting from Alaska, stretches far away to Japan, as if America were extending a friendly hand to Asia. This is the most general aspect. There are details specially disclosing maritime advantages and approaches to the sea which properly belong to this preliminary sketch. According to accurate estimates the coast line, including bays and islands, is not less than eleven thousand two hundred and seventy miles. In the Aleutian range, besides innumerable islets and rocks, there are not less than fifty-five islands exceeding three miles in length; there are seven exceeding forty miles, with Ounimak, which is the largest, exceeding seventy-three miles. In our part of Behring sea there are five considerable islands, the largest of which is St. Lawrence, being more than ninety-six miles long. Add to all these the group south of the peninsula of Alaska,

4

including the Shumagins and the magnificent island of Kodiak, and then the Sitkan group, being archipelago added to archipelago, and the whole together constituting the geographical complement to the West Indies, so that the northwest of the continent answers archipelago for archipelago to the southeast.

The title of Russia to all these possessions is derived from prior discovery, which is the admitted title by which all European Powers have held in North and South America, unless we except what England acquired by conquest from France; but here the title of France was derived from prior discovery. Russia, shut up in a distant interior and struggling with barbarism, was scarcely known to the other Powers at the time they were lifting their flags in the western hemisphere. At a later day the same powerful genius which made her known as an empire set in motion the enterprise by which these possessions were opened to her dominion. Peter the Great, himself a ship-builder and a reformer, who had worked in the ship-yards of England and Holland, was curious to know if Asia and America were separated by the sea, or if they constituted one undivided body with different names, like Europe and Asia. To obtain this information he wrote with his own hand the following instructions, and ordered his chief admiral to see them carried into execution:

"One or two boats with decks to be built at Kamtschatka, or at any other convenient place, with which inquiry should be made in relation to the northerly coasts, to see whether they were not contiguous with America, since their end was not known; and this done, they should see whether they could not somewhere find an harbor belonging to Europeans or an European ship. They should likewise set apart some men who should inquire after the name and situation of the coasts discovered. Of all this an exact journal should be kept, with which they should return to Petersburg."—*Müller's Voyages from Asia to America,* by Jeffreys, p. 45.

The Czar died in the winter of 1725; but the Empress Catharine, faithful to the desires of her husband, did not allow this work to be neglected. Vitus Behring, a Dane by birth, and a navigator of some experience, was made commander. The place of embarkation was on the other side of the Asiatic continent. Taking with him officers and ship-builders the navigator left St. Petersburg by land 5th February, 1725, and commenced the preliminary journey across Siberia, northern Asia, and the sea of Okhotsk to the coast of Kamtschatka, which they reached after infinite hardships and delays, sometimes with dogs for horses, and sometimes supporting life by eating leather bags, straps, and shoes. More than three years were passed in this toilsome and perilous journey to the place of embarkation. At last on the 20th of July, 1728, the party was able to set sail in a small vessel, called the Gabriel, and described as "like the packet-boats used in the Baltick." Steering in a northeasterly direction, Behring passed a large island, which

he called St. Lawrence from the saint on whose day it was seen. This island, which is included in the present cession, may be considered as the first point in Russian discovery, as it is also the first outpost of the North American continent. Continuing northward, and hugging the Asiatic coast, Behring turned back only when he thought he had reached the northeastern extremity of Asia, and was satisfied that the two continents were separated from each other. He did not penetrate further north than 67° 30'.

In his voyage Behring was struck by the absence of such great and high waves, as, in other places, are common to the open sea, and he observed fir trees swimming in the water, although they were unknown on the Asiatic coast. Relations of inhabitants, in harmony with these indications, pointed to "a country at no great distance toward the east." His work was still incomplete, and the navigator before returning home put forth again for this discovery, but without success. By another dreary land journey he made his way back to St. Petersburg in March, 1730, after an absence of five years. Something was accomplished for Russian discovery, and his own fame was engraved on the maps of the world. The straits through which he sailed now bear his name, as also does the expanse of sea which he traversed on his way to the straits.

The spirit of discovery continued at St. Petersburg. A Cossack chief undertaking to conquer the obstinate natives on the northeastern coast, proposed also "to discover the pretended country on the Frozen sea." He was killed by an arrow before his enterprise was completed. Little is known of the result; but it is stated that the navigator whom he had selected, by name Gwosdew, in 1730 succeeded in reaching a "strange coast" between sixty-five and sixty-six degrees of north latitude, where he saw people, but could not speak with them for want of an interpreter. This must have been the coast of North America, and not far from the group of islands in Behring straits, through which the present boundary passes, separating the United States from Russia, and America from Asia.

The desire of the Russian Government to get behind the curtain increased. Behring volunteered to undertake the discoveries that remained to be made. He was created a commodore, and his old lieutenants were created captains. The Senate, the Admiralty, and the Academy of Sciences at St. Petersburg all united in the enterprise. Several academicians were appointed to report on the natural history of the coasts visited, among whom was Steller, the naturalist, said to be "immortal" from this association. All of these, with a numerous body of officers, journeyed across Siberia, northern Asia, and the sea of Okhotsk, to Kamtschatka, as Behring had journeyed before. Though ordered in 1732, the expedition was not able to leave the western coast until 4th June, 1741, when two well-appointed ships set sail in company "to discover the continent of America." One of these, called the St. Paul, was under Commodore Behring; the other, called the St. Peter, was under Captain Tschirikow. For some time the two kept together; but in a violent storm and fog they were separated, when each continued the expedition alone.

Behring first saw the continent of North America on 18th July, 1741, in latitude 58° 28'. Looking at it from a distance "the country had terrible high mountains that were covered with snow." Two days later he anchored in a sheltered bay near a point which he called from the saint day on which he saw it, Cape St. Elias. He was in the shadow of Mount St. Elias. On landing he found deserted huts, fire-places, hewn wood, household furniture, an arrow, edge-tools of copper with "store of red salmon." Here also several birds unknown in Siberia were noticed by the faithful Steller, among which was the blue jay, of a peculiar species, now called by his name. Steering northward, Behring found himself constrained by the elbow in the coast to turn westward, and then in a southerly direction. Hugging the shore, his voyage was constantly arrested by islands without number, among which he zigzagged to find his way. Several times he landed. On one of these occasions he saw natives, who wore "upper garments of whale's guts, breeches of seal-skins, caps of the skins of sea lions, adorned with various feathers, especially those of hawks." These "Americans" as they are called were fishermen, without bows and arrows. They regaled the Russians with "whale's flesh," but declined strong drink. One of them, on receiving a cup of brandy, "spit it out again as soon as he tasted it and cried aloud, as if complaining to his countrymen how ill he had been used." This was on one of the Shumagin islands, near the southern coast of the peninsula of Alaska.

Meanwhile, the other solitary ship, proceeding on its way, had sighted the same coast 15th July, 1741, in the latitude of 56°. Anchoring at some distance from the steep and rocky cliffs before him, Tschirikow sent his mate with the long boat and ten of his best men, provided with small-arms and a brass cannon, to inquire into the nature of the country and to obtain fresh water. The long boat disappeared in a small wooded bay, and was never seen again. Thinking it might have been damaged in landing the captain sent his boatswain with the small boat and carpenters well armed to furnish necessary assistance. The small boat disappeared also, and was never seen again. At the same time great smoke was observed continually ascending from the shore. Shortly afterwards two boats filled with natives sallied forth and lay at some distance from the vessel, when, crying "Agai, Agai," they put back to the shore. Sorrowfully the Russian navigator turned away, not knowing the fate of his comrades and unable to help them. This was not far from Sitka.

Such was the first discovery of these northwestern coasts; and such are the first recorded glimpses of the aboriginal inhabitants. The two navigators had different fortunes. Tschirikow, deprived of his boats, and therefore unable to land, hurried home. Adverse winds and storms interfered. He supplied himself with fresh water only by distilling the ocean or pressing rain from the sails. But at last on the 9th October he reached Kamtschatka, with his ship's company of seventy diminished to forty-nine. During this time Behring was driven, like Ulysses, on the uncertain waves. A single tempest raged for seventeen days, so that Andrew Hosselberg, the ancient pilot, who had known the sea for fifty years, declared that he had seen nothing like it in his life. Scurvy came with its disheartening horrors. The commodore himself was a sufferer. Rigging broke. Cables snapped. Anchors were lost. At last the tempest-tossed vessel was cast upon a desert island, then without a name, where the commodore, sheltered in a ditch and half-covered with sand as a protection against cold, died 8th December, 1741. His body after his decease was "scraped out of the ground" and buried on this island, which is called by his name, and constitutes an outpost of the Asiatic continent. Thus the Russian navigator, after the discovery of America, died in Asia. Russia, by the recent demarcation, does not fail to retain his last resting-place among her possessions.

TITLE OF RUSSIA.

For some time after these expeditions, by which Russia achieved the palm of discovery, imperial enterprise slumbered in those seas. The knowledge already acquired was continued and confirmed only by private individuals, who were led there in quest of furs. In 1745 the Aleutian islands were discovered by an adventurer in search of sea otters. In successive voyages all these islands were visited for similar purposes. Among these was Ounalaska, the principal of the group of Fox islands, constituting a continuation of the Aleutian islands, whose inhabitants and productions were minutely described. In 1768 private enterprise was superseded by an expedition ordered by the Empress Catharine, which, leaving Kamtschatka, explored this whole archipelago and the peninsula of Alaska, which to the islanders stood for the whole continent. Shortly afterwards all these discoveries, beginning with those of Behring and Tschirikow, were verified by the great English navigator, Captain Cook. In 1778 he sailed along the northwestern coast, "near where Tschirikow anchored in 1741;" then again in sight of mountains "wholly covered with snow from the highest summit down to the sea-coast," "with the summit of an elevated mountain above the horizon," which he supposed to be the Mount St. Elias of Behring; then by the very anchorage of Behring; then among the islands through which Behring zigzagged, and along the coast by the island of St. Lawrence until arrested by ice. If any doubt existed with regard to Russian discoveries it was removed by the authentic report of this navigator, who shed such a flood of light upon the geography of this region.

Such from the beginning is the title of Russia, dating at least from 1741. The coast of British Columbia, next below, was discovered by Vancouver in 1790, and that of Oregon, still further down, by Gray, who, sailing from Boston in 1789, entered the Columbia river in 1790; so that the title of Russia is the earliest on the northwestern coast. I have not stopped to quote volume and page, but I beg to be understood as following approved authorities, and I refer especially to the Russian work of Müller, already cited, on the *Voyages from Asia to America*; the volume of Coxe on *Russian Discoveries* with its supplement on the *Comparative View of Russian Discoveries*; the volume of Sir John Barrow, on *Arctic Voyages*; Burney's *Russian and Northeastern Voyages*; and the third voyage of Captain Cook, unhappily interrupted by his tragical death from the natives of the Sandwich islands, but not until after his exploration of this coast.

There were at least four other Russian expeditions by which this title was confirmed, if it needed any confirmation. The first was ordered by the Empress Catharine in 1785. It was under the command of Commodore Billings, an Englishman in the service of Russia, and was narrated from the original papers by Martin Sauer, secretary of the expedition. In the instructions from the Admiralty at St. Petersburg the Commodore was directed to take possession of "such coasts and islands as he shall first discover, whether inhabited or not, that cannot be disputed, and are not yet subject to any European Power, with consent of the inhabitants, if any," and this was to be accomplished by setting up "posts marked with the arms of Russia, with letters indicating the time of sovereignty, a short account of the people, their voluntary submission to the Russian sovereignty, and that this was done under the glorious reign of the great Catharine the Second." (Billings's Northern Russia, Appendix.) The next was in 1803, in the interest of the Russian American Company. There were two ships, one under the command of Captain Lisiansky, and the other of Captain Krusenstern, of the Russian navy. It was the first voyage round the world by the Russian Government, and lasted three years. During its progress these ships visited separately the northwest coast of America, and especially Sitka and the island of Kodiak. Still another enterprise organized by the celebrated minister Count Romanzoff, and at his expense, left Russia in 1815, under the command of Lieutenant Kotzebue, an officer of the Russian navy, and son of the German dramatist, whose assassination darkened the return of the son from his long voyage. It is enough for the present to say of this expedition that it has left its honorable traces on the coast even as far as the Frozen ocean. There remains the enterprise of Lütke, at the time captain, and afterward admiral in the Russian navy, which was a voyage round the world, embracing especially the Russian possessions, commenced in 1826, and described in French with instructive fullness. With him sailed the German naturalist Kittlitz, who has done so much to illustrate the natural history of this region.

A FRENCH ASPIRATION ON THIS COAST.

So little was the Russian title recognized for some time, that when the unfortunate expedition of La Pérouse, with the frigates Boussole and Astrolabe, stopped on this coast in 1787, he did not hesitate to consider the friendly harbor, in latitude 58° 36′, where he was moored as open to permanent occupation. Describing this harbor, which he named *Port des Francais*, as sheltered behind a breakwater of rocks, with a calm sea and with a mouth sufficiently large, he says that nature seemed to have created at this extremity of the world a port like that of Toulon but vaster in plan and accommodation; and then considering that it had never been discovered before, that it was situated thirty-three leagues northwest of Remedios, the limit of Spanish navigation, about two hundred and eighty-four leagues from Nootka and a hundred leagues from Prince William sound, the mariner records his judgment that "if the French Government had any project of a factory on this coast no nation could have the slightest right to oppose it." (La Pérouse, Voyage, Tom. 2, p. 147.) Thus quietly was Russia dislodged. The frigates sailed further on their voyage and never returned to France. Their fate was unknown, until after fruitless search and the lapse of a generation their shipwrecked hulls were accidentally found on a desert island of the southern Pacific. The unfinished journal of La Pérouse recording his visit to this coast had been sent overland, by way of Kamtschatka and Siberia, to France, where it was published by a decree of the National Assembly, thus making known his supposed discovery and his aspiration.

EARLY SPANISH CLAIM.

Spain also has been a claimant. In 1775 Bodega, a Spanish navigator, seeking new opportunities to plant the Spanish flag, reached the parallel of 58° on this coast, not far from Sitka; but this supposed discovery was not followed by any immediate assertion of dominion. The universal aspiration of Spain had embraced this whole region even at an early day, and shortly after the return of Bodega another enterprise was equipped to verify the larger claim, being nothing less than the original title as discoverer of the straits between America and Asia and of the conterminous continent under the name of Anian. This curious episode is not out of place in this brief history. It has two branches: one concerning early maps on which straits are represented between America and Asia under the name of

Anian; the other concerning a pretended attempt by a Spanish navigator at an early day to find these straits.

There can be no doubt that early maps exist with northwestern straits marked Anian. There are two in the Congressional Library in atlases of the years 1717 and 1680; but these are of a date comparatively modern. Engel, in his *Mémoires Géographiques*, mentions several earlier, which he believes to be genuine. There is one purporting to be by Zaltieri, and bearing date 1566, an authentic pen-and-ink copy of which is now before me from the collection of our own Coast Survey. On this very interesting map, which is without latitude or longitude, the western coast of the continent is delineated with straits separating it from Asia not unlike Behring straits in outline, and with the name in Italian *Stretto di Anian*. Southward the coast has a certain conformity with what is now known to exist. Below the straits is an indentation corresponding to Bristol bay; then a peninsula somewhat broader than that of Alaska; then comes the elbow of the coast; then lower down three islands, not unlike Sitka, Queen Charlotte, and Vancouver; and then, further south, is the peninsula of Lower California. Sometimes the story of Anian is explained by the voyage of the Portuguese navigator Caspar de Cortereal in 1500–1505, when, on reaching Hudson bay in quest of a passage round America, he imagined that he had found it, and proceeded to name his discovery "in honor of two brothers who accompanied him." Very soon maps began to record the straits of Anian; but this does not explain the substantial conformity of the early delineation with the reality, which seems truly remarkable.

The other branch of inquiry is more easily disposed of. This turns on a Spanish document entitled "Relation of the Discovery of the Strait of Anian, made by me Captain Lorenzo Ferren Maldonado," purporting to be written at the time, although it did not see the light till 1781, when it was published in Spain, and shortly afterward became the subject of a memoir before the French Academy. If this early account of a northwest passage from the Atlantic to the Pacific were authentic the whole question would be settled, but recent geographers indignantly discard it as a barefaced imposture. Clearly Spain once regarded it otherwise; for her Government in 1789 sent out an expedition "to discover the strait by which Maldonado was supposed to have passed in 1588 from the coast of Labrador to the Great Ocean." The expedition was not successful, and nothing more has been heard of any claim from this pretended discovery. The story of Maldonado has taken its place in the same category with that of Munchausen.

REASONS FOR THIS CESSION BY RUSSIA.

Turning from this question of title, which time and testimony have already settled, I meet the inquiry, why does Russia part with possessions thus associated with the reign of her greatest emperor and filling an important chapter of geographical history? On this head I have no information which is not open to others. But I do not forget that the first Napoleon in parting with Louisiana was controlled by three several considerations: first, he needed the purchase-money for his treasury; secondly, he was unwilling to leave this distant unguarded territory a prey to Great Britain in the event of hostilities which seemed at hand; and thirdly, he was glad, according to his own remarkable language, "to establish forever the power of the United States and give to England a maritime rival destined to humble her pride." Such is the record of history. Perhaps a similar record may be made hereafter with regard to the present cession. It is sometimes imagined that Russia, with all her great empire, is financially poor, so that these few millions may not be unimportant to her. It is by foreign loans that her railroads have been built and her wars have been aided. All, too, must see that in those "coming events," which now more than ever "cast their shadows before," it will be for her advantage not to hold outlying possessions from which thus far she has obtained no income commensurate with the possible expense for their protection. Perhaps, like a wrestler, she now strips for the contest, which I trust sincerely may be averted. Besides I cannot doubt that her enlightened emperor, who has given pledges to civilization by an unsurpassed act of Emancipation, would join the first Napoleon in a desire to enhance the maritime power of the United States.

These general considerations are reënforced when we call to mind the little influence which Russia has thus far been able to exercise in this region. Though possessing dominion over it for more than a century this gigantic Power has not been more genial or productive there than the soil itself. Her government there is little more than a name or a shadow. It is not even a skeleton. It is hardly visible. Its only representative is a fur company, to which has been added latterly an ice company. The immense country is without form and without light; without activity and without progress. Distant from the imperial capital, and separated from the huge bulk of Russian empire, it does not share the vitality of a common country. Its life is solitary and feeble. Its settlements are only encampments or lodges. Its fisheries are only a petty perquisite, belonging to local or personal adventurers rather than to the commerce of nations.

In these statements I follow the record. So little were these possessions regarded during the last century that they were scarcely recognized as a component part of the empire. I have now before me an authentic map, published by the Academy of Sciences at St. Petersburg in 1776, and reproduced at London in 1787, entitled "General Map of the Russian

Empire," where you will look in vain for Russian America, unless we except that link of the Aleutian chain nearest to Asia, which appears to have been incorporated under the Empress Anna at the same time with Siberia. (See Coxe's Russian Discoveries.) Alexander Humboldt, whose insight into geography was unerring, in his great work on New Spain, published in 1811, after stating that he is able from official documents to give the position of the Russian factories on the American continent, says that they are "nothing but sheds and cabins employed as magazines of furs." He remarks further that "the larger part of these small Russian colonies do not communicate with each other except by sea," and then, putting us on our guard not to expect too much from a name, he proceeds to say that "the new denomination of *Russian America* or *Russian possessions* on the new continent must not make us think that the coasts of Behring's Basin, the peninsula of Alaska, or the country of Tchuktchi have become *Russian provinces* in the sense given to this word, when we speak of the Spanish provinces of Sonora or New Biscay." (Humboldt, *Essai Politique sur La Nouvelle Espagne*, Tom. I, pp. 344, 345.) Here is a distinction between the foothold of Spain in California and the foothold of Russia in North America, which will at least illustrate the slender power of the latter in this region.

In ceding possessions so little within the sphere of her empire, embracing more than one hundred nations or tribes, Russia gives up no part of herself, and even if she did the considerable price paid, the alarm of war which begins to fill our ears, and the sentiments of friendship declared for the United States would explain the transaction.

THE NEGOTIATION, IN ITS ORIGIN AND COMPLETION.

I am not able to say when the idea of this cession first took shape. I have heard that it was as long ago as the administration of Mr. Polk. It is within my knowledge that the Russian Government was sounded on the subject during the administration of Mr. Buchanan. This was done through Mr. Gwin, at the time Senator of California, and Mr. Appleton, Assistant Secretary of State. For this purpose the former had more than one interview with the Russian minister at Washington some time in December, 1859, in which, while professing to speak for the President unofficially, he represented "that Russia was too far off to make the most of these possessions; and that, as we are near, we can derive more from them." In reply to an inquiry of the Russian minister Mr. Gwin said that "the United States could go as high as $5,000,000 for the purchase," on which the former made no comment. Mr. Appleton, on another occasion, said to the minister that "the President thought that the acquisition would be very profitable to the States on the Pacific; that he was ready to follow it up, but wished to know in advance if

Russia was ready to cede; that if she were, he would confer with his Cabinet and influential members of Congress." All this was unofficial; but it was promptly communicated to the Russian Government, who seem to have taken it into careful consideration. Prince Gortschakow, in a dispatch which reached here early in the summer of 1860, said that "the offer was not what might have been expected; but that it merited mature reflection; that the Minister of Finance was about to inquire into the condition of these possessions, after which Russia would be in a condition to treat." The prince added for himself that "he was by no means satisfied personally that it would be for the interest of Russia politically to alienate these possessions; that the only consideration which could make the scales incline that way would be the prospect of great financial advantages; but that the sum of $5,000,000 does not seem in any way to represent the real value of these possessions," and he concluded by asking the minister to tell Mr. Appleton and Senator Gwin that the sum offered was not considered "an equitable equivalent." The subject was submerged by the presidential election which was approaching, and then by the Rebellion. It will be observed that this attempt was at a time when politicians who believed in the perpetuity of slavery still had power. Mr. Buchanan was President, and he employed as his intermediary a known sympathizer with slavery, who shortly afterward became a rebel. Had Russia been willing, it is doubtful if this controlling interest would have sanctioned any acquisition too far north for slavery.

Meanwhile the Rebellion was brought to an end, and peaceful enterprise was renewed, which on the Pacific coast was directed toward the Russian possessions. Our people there wishing new facilities to obtain fish, fur, and ice, sought the intervention of the national Government. The Legislature of Washington Territory, in the winter of 1866, adopted a memorial to the President of the United States, entitled "in reference to the cod and other fisheries," as follows:

To his Excellency ANDREW JOHNSON,
President of the United States:

Your memorialists, the Legislative Assembly of Washington Territory, beg leave to show that abundance of codfish, halibut, and salmon of excellent quality have been found along the shores of the Russian possessions. Your memorialists respectfully request your Excellency to obtain such rights and privileges of the Government of Russia as will enable our fishing vessels to visit the ports and harbors of its possessions to the end that fuel, water, and provisions may be easily obtained, that our sick and disabled fishermen may obtain sanitary assistance, together with the privilege of curing fish and repairing vessels in need of repairs. Your memorialists further request that the Treasury Department be instructed to forward to the collector of customs of this Puget sound district such fishing licenses, abstract journals, and log-books as will enable our hardy fishermen to obtain the bounties now provided and paid to the fisherman in the Atlantic States. Your memorialists finally pray your Excellency to employ such ships as may be spared from the Pacific naval fleet in exploring and surveying the fishing banks known to navigators to exist along the Pacific coast from the Cortes bank to Behring straits, and as in duty bound your memorialists will ever pray.

Passed the House of Representatives January 10, 1866.

EDWARD ELDRIDGE,
Speaker House of Representatives.

Passed the Council January 13, 1866.

HARVEY K. HINES,
President of the Council.

This memorial on its presentation to the President in February, 1866, was referred to the Secretary of State, by whom it was communicated to Mr. de Stoeckl, the Russian minister, with remarks on the importance of some early and comprehensive arrangement between the two Powers in order to prevent the growth of difficulties, especially from the fisheries in that region.

Shortly afterwards another influence was felt. Mr. Cole, who had been recently elected to the Senate from California, acting in behalf of certain persons in that State, sought to obtain from the Russian Government a license or franchise to gather furs in a portion of its American possessions. The charter of the Russian American Company was about to expire. This company had already underlet to the Hudson Bay Company all its franchise on the main land between 54° 40' and Mount St. Elias; and now it was proposed that an American company, holding direct from the Russian Government, should be substituted for the latter. The mighty Hudson Bay Company, with its headquarters in London, was to give way to an American Company with its headquarters in California. Among the letters on this subject addressed to Mr. Cole and now before me is one dated at San Francisco, April 10, 1866, in which this scheme is developed as follows:

"There is at the present time a good chance to organize a fur trading company to trade between the United States and the Russian possessions in America, and as the charter formerly granted to the Hudson Bay Company has expired this would be the opportune moment to start in." * * * * "I should think that by a little management this charter could be obtained from the Russian Government for ourselves, as I do not think they are very willing to renew the charter of the Hudson Bay Company, and I think they would give the preference to an American company, especially if the company should pay to the Russian Government five per cent. on the gross proceeds of their transactions, and also aid in civilizing and ameliorating the condition of the Indians by employing missionaries, if required by the Russian Government. For the faithful performance of the above we ask a charter for the term of twenty-five years, to be renewed for the same length of time, if the Russian Government finds the company deserving. The charter to invest us with the right of trading in all the country between the British American line and the Russian archipelago." * * * * "Remember, we wish for the same charter as was formerly granted to the Hudson Bay Company, and we offer in return more than they did."

Another correspondent of Mr. Cole, under date of San Francisco, 17th September, 1866, wrote as follows:

"I have talked with a man who has been on the coast and in the trade for ten years past, and he says it is much more valuable than I have supposed, and I think it very important to obtain it if possible."

The Russian minister at Washington, whom Mr. Cole saw repeatedly upon this subject,

was not authorized to act, and the latter, after conference with the Department of State, was induced to address Mr. Clay, minister of the United States at St. Petersburg, who laid the application before the Russian Government. This was an important step. A letter from Mr. Clay, dated at St. Petersburg as late as 1st February, 1867, makes the following revelation:

"The Russian Government has already ceded away its rights in Russian America for a term of years, and the Russo-American Company has also ceded the same to the Hudson Bay Company. This lease expires in June next, and the president of the Russo-American Company tells me that they have been in correspondence with the Hudson Bay Company about a renewal of the lease for another term of twenty-five or thirty years. Until he receives a definite answer he cannot enter into negotiations with us or your California company. My opinion is that if he can get off with the Hudson Bay Company he will do so, when we can make some arrangements with the Russo-American Company."

Some time had elapsed since the original attempt of Mr. Gwin, also a Senator from California, and it is probable that the Russian Government had obtained information which enabled it to see its way more clearly. It will be remembered that Prince Gortschakow had promised an inquiry, and it is known that in 1861 Captain Lieutenant Golowin, of the Russian navy, made a detailed report on these possessions. Mr. Cole had the advantage of his predecessor. There is reason to believe, also, that the administration of the fur company had not been entirely satisfactory, so that there were well-founded hesitations with regard to the renewal of its franchise. Meanwhile, in October, 1866, Mr. de Stoeckl, who had long been the Russian minister at Washington, and enjoyed in a high degree the confidence of our Government, returned home on a leave of absence, promising his best exertions to promote good relations between the two countries. While he was at St. Petersburg the applications from the United States were under consideration; but the Russian Government was disinclined to any minor arrangement of the character proposed. Obviously something like a crisis was at hand with regard to these possessions. The existing government was not adequate. The franchises granted there were about to terminate. Something must be done. As Mr. de Stoeckl was leaving in February to return to his post the Archduke Constantine, the brother and chief adviser of the emperor, handed him a map with the lines in our Treaty marked upon it, and told him he might treat for this cession. The minister arrived in Washington early in March. A negotiation was opened at once with our Government. Final instructions were received by the Atlantic cable from St. Petersburg on the 29th March, and at four o'clock on the morning of the 30th March this important Treaty was signed by Mr. Seward on the part of the United States and by Mr. de Stoeckl on the part of Russia.

Few treaties have been conceived, initiated, prosecuted, and completed in so simple a manner without protocols or dispatches. The whole negotiation will be seen in its result, unless we accept two brief notes, which constitute all that passed between the negotiators. These have an interest general and special, and I conclude the history of this transaction by reading them:

DEPARTMENT OF STATE,
WASHINGTON, *March 23,* 1867.

SIR: With reference to the proposed convention between our respective Governments for a cession by Russia of her American territory to the United States, I have the honor to acquaint you that I must insist upon that clause in the sixth article of the draft which declares the cession to be free and unincumbered by any reservations, privileges, franchises, grants, or possessions by any associated companies, whether corporate or incorporate, Russian or any other, &c., and must regard it as an ultimatum. With the President's approval, however, I will add $200,000 to the consideration money on that account.

I avail myself of this occasion to offer to you a renewed assurance of my most distinguished consideration. WILLIAM H. SEWARD.
Mr. EDWARD DE STOECKL, &c., &c., &c.

[Translation.]
WASHINGTON, *March* 17 | 29, 1867.

MR. SECRETARY OF STATE: I have the honor to inform you that by a telegram dated 16 | 28th of this month from St. Petersburg, Prince Gortchakow informs me that his Majesty the Emperor of all the Russias gives his consent to the cession of the Russian possessions on the American continent to the United States for the stipulated sum of $7,200,000 in gold, and that his Majesty the Emperor invests me with full powers to negotiate and sign the treaty.

Please accept, Mr. Secretary of State, the assurance of my very high consideration. STOECKL.
To Hon. WILLIAM H. SEWARD,
Secretary of State of the United States.

THE TREATY.

The Treaty begins with the declaration that "the United States of America and his Majesty the Emperor of all the Russias, being desirous of strengthening, if possible, the good understanding which exists between them," have appointed plenipotentiaries, who have proceeded to sign articles, wherein it is stipulated on behalf of Russia that "his Majesty the Emperor of all the Russias agrees to cede to the United States by this convention, immediately upon the exchange of the ratifications thereof, all the territory and dominion now possessed by his said Majesty on the continent of America and in the adjacent islands, the same being contained within the geographical limits herein set forth;" and it is stipulated on behalf of the United States that "in consideration of the cession aforesaid the United States agree to pay at the Treasury in Washington, within ten months after the ratification of this convention, to the diplomatic representative or other agent of his Majesty the Emperor of all the Russias duly authorized to receive the same, $7,200,000 in gold." The ratifications are to be exchanged within three months from the date of the Treaty, or sooner, if possible.

Beyond the consideration founded on the desire of "strengthening the good understanding" between the two countries, there is the pecuniary consideration already mentioned, which underwent a change in the progress of the negotiation. The sum of seven millions was originally agreed upon; but when it was understood that there was a fur company and also an ice company enjoying monopolies under the existing government, it was thought best that these should be extinguished, in consideration of which our Government added $200,000 to the purchase money, and the Russian Government in formal terms declared "the cession of territory and dominion to be free and unincumbered by any reservations, privileges, franchises, grants, or possessions, by any associated companies, whether corporate or incorporate, or by any parties, except merely private individual property-holders." Thus the United States receive this cession free of all incumbrances, so far at least as Russia is in a condition to make it. The Treaty proceeds to say, that "the cession hereby made conveys all the rights, franchises, and privileges now belonging to Russia in the said territory or dominion and appurtenances thereto." In other words, Russia conveys all that she has to convey.

QUESTIONS ARISING UNDER THE TREATY.

There are questions not unworthy of attention, which arise under the treaty between Russia and Great Britain, fixing the eastern limits of these possessions, and conceding certain privileges to the latter Power. By this treaty, signed at St. Petersburg 28th February, 1825, after fixing the boundaries between the Russian and British possessions, it is provided that "for the space of *ten years* the vessels of the two Powers, or those belonging to their respective subjects, shall mutually be at liberty to frequent, without any hinderance whatever, all the inland seas, gulfs, havens, and creeks on the coast for the purpose of fishing and of trading with the natives;" and also that "for the space of *ten years* the port of Sitka or Novo Archangelsk shall be open to the commerce and vessels of British subjects." (Hertslet's Commercial Treaties, vol. 2, p 365.) In the same Treaty it is also provided that "the subjects of his Britannic Majesty, from whatever quarter they may arrive, whether from the ocean or from the interior of the continent, shall *forever* enjoy the right of navigating freely and without any hinderance whatever all the rivers and streams which in their course toward the Pacific ocean may cross the line of demarcation." (*Ibid.*) Afterwards a Treaty of Commerce and Navigation between Russia and Great Britain was signed at St. Petersburg 11th January, 1843, subject to be terminated on notice from either party at the expiration of ten years, in which it is provided that "in regard to commerce and navigation in the Russian possessions on the northwest coast of America the convention of 28th February, 1825, continues in force." (*Ibid.*, vol. 6, p. 767.) Then ensued the Crimean war between Russia and Great Britain, effacing or suspending treaties. Afterwards another Treaty of Commerce and Navigation was signed at St. Petersburg 12th January, 1859, subject to be terminated on notice from either party at the expiration of ten years, which repeats the last provision. (*Ibid.*, vol. 10, p 1063.)

Thus we have three different stipulations on the part of Russia; one opening seas, gulfs, and havens on the Russian coast to British subjects for fishing and trading with the natives; the second making Sitka a free port to British subjects; and the third making British rivers which flow through the Russian possessions forever free to British navigation. Do the United States succeed to these stipulations?

Among these I make a distinction in favor of the last, which by its language is declared to be "forever," and may have been in the nature of an equivalent at the settlement of the boundaries between the two Powers. But whatever may be its terms or its origin it is obvious that it is nothing but a declaration of public law as it has always been expounded by the United States and is now recognized on the continent of Europe. While pleading with Great Britain in 1826 for the free navigation of the St. Lawrence Mr. Clay, who was at the time Secretary of State, said that "the American Government did not mean to contend for any principle the benefit of which, in analogous circumstances, it would deny to Great Britain." (Wheaton's Elements of International Law, part 2, cap. 4.) During the same year Mr. Gallatin, our minister in London, when negotiating with Great Britain for the adjustment of our boundaries on the Pacific, proposed that "if the line should cross any of the branches of the Columbia at points from which they are navigable by boats to the main stream the navigation of both branches and of the main stream should be perpetually free and common to the people of both nations." At an earlier day the United States made the same claim with regard to the Mississippi, and asserted as a general principle that "if the right of the upper inhabitants to descend the stream was in any case obstructed it was an act by a stronger society against a weaker, condemned by the judgment of mankind." (*Ibid.*) By these admissions our country is estopped, even if the public law of the European continent, first declared at Vienna with regard to the Rhine, did not offer an example which we cannot afford to reject. I rejoice to believe that on this occasion we shall apply to Great Britain the generous rule which from the beginning we have claimed for ourselves.

The two other stipulations are different in character. They are not declared to be "forever," and do not stand on any principle of public law. Even if subsisting now they cannot be onerous. I doubt much if they are subsisting now. In succeeding to the Russian possessions it does not follow that the United States succeed to ancient obligations assumed by Russia, as if, according to a phrase of the common law, they are "covenants running with the land." If these stipulations are in the nature of *servitudes* they depend for their duration on the sovereignty of Russia, and are

personal or *national* rather than *territorial.* So at least I am inclined to believe. But it is hardly profitable to speculate on a point of so little practical value. Even if "running with the land" these *servitudes* can be terminated at the expiration of ten years from the last treaty by a notice, which equitably the United States may give, so as to take effect on the 12th January, 1869. Meanwhile, during this brief period, it will be easy by act of Congress in advance to limit importations at Sitka, so that this "free port" shall not be made the channel or doorway by which British goods may be introduced into the United States free of duty.

GENERAL CONSIDERATIONS ON THE TREATY.

From this survey of the Treaty, as seen in its origin and the questions under it, I might pass at once to a survey of the possessions which have been conveyed; but there are other matters of a more general character which present themselves at this stage and challenge the judgment. These concern nothing less than the unity, power, and grandeur of the Republic, with the extension of its dominion and its institutions. Such considerations, where not entirely inapplicable, are apt to be controlling. I do not doubt that they will in a great measure determine the fate of this treaty with the American people. They are patent, and do not depend on research or statistics. To state them is enough.

Advantages to the Pacific Coast.

(1.) Foremost in order, if not in importance, I put the desires of our fellow-citizens on the Pacific coast, and the special advantages which they will derive from this enlargement of boundary. They were the first to ask for it, and will be the first to profit by it. While others knew the Russian possessions only on the map they knew them practically in their resources. While others were still indifferent they were planning how to appropriate Russian peltries and fisheries. This is attested by the resolutions of the Legislature of Washington Territory; also by the exertions at different times of two Senators from California, who, differing in political sentiments and in party relations, took the initial steps which ended in this Treaty.

These well-known desires were founded, of course, on supposed advantages; and here experience and neighborhood were prompters. Since 1854 the people of California have received their ice from the fresh-water lakes in the island of Kodiak, not far westward from Mount St. Elias. Later still their fishermen have searched the waters about the Aleutians and the Shumagins, commencing a promising fishery. Others have proposed to substitute themselves to the Hudson Bay Company in their franchise on the coast. But all are looking to the Orient, as in the time of Columbus, although like him they sail to the West. To them China and Japan, those ancient realms of fabulous wealth, are the Indies. To draw this commerce to the Pacific coast is no new idea. It haunted the early navigators. Meares, the Englishman, whose voyage in the intervening seas was in 1789, closes his volumes with an essay, entitled "The trade between the northwest coast of America and China," in the course of which he dwells on the "great and very valuable source of commerce" afforded by China as "forming a chain of trade between Hudson bay, Canada, and the northwest coast," and then he exhibits on the American side the costly furs of the sea otter, which are still so much prized in China; "mines which are known to lie between the latitudes 40° and 60°, north;" and also an "inexhaustible supply" of ginseng, for which there is still such a demand in China that even Minnesota, at the headwaters of the Mississippi, supplies her contribution. His catalogue might be extended now.

As a practical illustration of this idea, it may be mentioned that for a long time most if not all the sea otter skins of this coast found their way to China, excluding even Russia herself. China was the best customer, and therefore Englishmen and Americans followed the Russian company in carrying these furs to her market, so that Pennant, the English naturalist, impressed by the peculiar advantages of this coast, exclaimed, "What a profitable trade with China might not a colony carry on were it possible to penetrate to that part of the country by means of rivers and lakes!" But under the present Treaty this coast is ours.

The absence of harbors at present belonging to the United States on the Pacific limits the outlets of the country. On that whole extent, from Panama to Puget's sound, the only harbor of any considerable value is San Francisco. Further north the harbors are abundant, and they are all nearer to the great marts of Japan and China. But San Francisco itself will be nearer by the way of the Aleutians than by Honolulu. The projection of maps is not always calculated to present an accurate idea of distances. From measurement on a globe it appears that a voyage from San Francisco to Hong Kong by the common way of the Sandwich islands is 7,140 miles, but by way of the Aleutian islands it is only 6,060 miles, being a saving of more than one thousand miles, with the enormous additional advantage of being obliged to carry much less coal. Of course a voyage from Sitka, or from Puget sound, the terminus of the Northern Pacific railroad, would be shorter still.

The advantages to the Pacific coast have two aspects, one domestic and the other foreign. Not only does the Treaty extend the coasting trade of California, Oregon, and Washington Territory northward, but it also extends the base of commerce with China and Japan.

To unite the east of Asia with the west of America is the aspiration of commerce now as when the English navigator recorded his voyage. Of course whatever helps this result is an advantage. The Pacific railroad is such an advantage, for, though running westward, it will be, when completed, a new highway to the East. This Treaty is another advantage, for nothing can be clearer than that the western coast must exercise an attraction which will be felt in China and Japan just in proportion as it is occupied by a commercial people communicating readily with the Atlantic and with Europe. This cannot be done without consequences not less important politically than commercially. Owing so much to the Union, the people there will be bound to it anew, and the national unity will receive another confirmation. Thus the whole country will be a gainer. So are we knit together that the advantages to the Pacific coast will contribute to the general welfare.

Extension of Dominion.

(2.) The extension of dominion is another consideration, calculated to captivate the public mind. Few are so cold or philosophical as to regard with insensibility a widening of the bounds of country. Wars have been regarded as successful when they have given a new territory. The discoverer who had planted the flag of his sovereign on a distant coast has been received as a conqueror. The ingratitude which was shown to Columbus during his later days was compensated by the epitaph that he had given a new world to Castile and Leon. His discoveries were continued by other navigators, and Spain girdled the earth with her possessions. Portugal, France, Holland, England, each followed the example of Spain and rejoiced in extended empire.

Our territorial acquisitions are among the landmarks of our history. In 1803 Louisiana, embracing the valley of the Mississippi, was acquired from France for fifteen million dollars. In 1819 Florida was acquired from Spain for three million dollars. In 1845 Texas was annexed without any purchase, but subsequently her debt was assumed to the amount of seven and a half million dollars. In 1848 California, New Mexico, and Utah were acquired from Mexico after war, and on payment of fifteen million dollars. In 1854 Arizona was acquired from Mexico for ten million dollars. And now it is proposed to acquire Russian America.

The passion for acquisition, which is so strong in the individual, is not less strong in the community. A nation seeks an outlying territory, as an individual seeks an outlying farm. The passion shows itself constantly. France, passing into Africa, has annexed Algeria. Spain set her face in the same direction, but without the same success. There are two great Powers with which annexation has become a habit. One is Russia, which from the time of Peter the Great has been moving her flag forward in every direction, so that on every side her limits have been extended. Even now the report comes that she is lifting her southern landmarks in Asia, so as to carry her boundary to India. The other annexationist is Great Britain, which from time to time adds another province to her Indian dominion. If the United States have from time to time added to their dominion they have only yielded to the universal passion, although I do not forget that the late Theodore Parker was accustomed to say that among all people the Anglo-Saxons were remarkable for "a greed of land." It was land, not gold, that aroused the Anglo-Saxon phlegm. I doubt, however, if this passion be stronger with us than with others, except, perhaps, that in a community where all participate in government the national sentiments are more active. It is common to the human family. There are few anywhere who could hear of a considerable accession of territory, obtained peacefully and honestly, without a pride of country, even if at certain moments the judgment hesitated. With an increased size on the map there is an increased consciousness of strength, and the citizen throbs anew as he traces the extending line.

Extension of Republican Institutions.

(3.) More than the extension of dominion is the extension of republican institutions, which is a traditional aspiration. It was in this spirit that Independence was achieved. In the name of Human Rights our fathers overthrew the kingly power, whose representative was George the Third. They set themselves openly against this form of government. They were against it for themselves, and offered their example to mankind. They were Roman in character, and turned to Roman lessons. With a cynical austerity the early Cato said that kings were "carnivorous animals," and at his instance the Roman Senate decreed that no king should be allowed within the gates of the city. A kindred sentiment, with less austerity of form, has been received from our fathers; but our city can be nothing less than the North American continent with its gates on all the surrounding seas.

John Adams, in the preface to his Defense of the American Constitution, written in London, where he resided at the time as minister, and dated January 1, 1787, at Grosvenor Square, the central seat of aristocratic fashion, after exposing the fabulous origin of the kingly power in contrast with the simple origin of our republican constitutions, thus for a moment lifts the curtain of the future: "Thirteen governments," he says plainly, "thus founded on the natural authority of the people alone, and without any pretense of miracle or mystery, and *which are destined to spread over the northern part of that whole quarter of the globe*, is a great point gained in favor of the rights of mankind." (John Adams's Works, vol. 4, p. 293.) Thus, according to this prophetic minister, even at that early day was the

destiny of the Republic manifest. It was to spread over the northern part of the American quarter of the globe; and it was to be a support to the rights of mankind.

By the text of our Constitution the United States are bound to guaranty a "republican form of government" to every State in this Union; but this obligation, which is only applicable at home, is an unquestionable indication of the national aspiration everywhere. The Republic is something more than a local policy; it is a general principle, not to be forgotten at any time, especially when the opportunity is presented of bringing an immense region within its influence. Elsewhere it has for the present failed; but on this account our example is more important. Who can forget the generous lament of Lord Byron, whose passion for ~~freedom~~ was not mitigated by his rank as an hereditary legislator of England, when he exclaims in memorable verse:

"The name of commonwealth is past and gone
O'er the three fractions of the groaning globe!"

Who can forget the salutation which the poet sends to the "one great clime," which, nursed in freedom, enjoys what he calls "the proud distinction" of not being confounded with other lands, ,

"Whose sons must bow them at a monarch's motion,
As if his senseless scepter were a wand!"

The present Treaty is a visible step in the occupation of the whole North American continent. As such it will be recognized by the world and accepted by the American people. But the Treaty involves something more. By it we dismiss one more monarch from this continent. One by one they have retired; first France; then Spain; then France again; and now Russia; all giving way to that absorbing Unity which is declared in the national motto, *E pluribus unum.*

Anticipation of Great Britain.

(4.) Another motive to this acquisition may be found in a desire to anticipate the imagined schemes or necessities of Great Britain. With regard to all these I confess my doubts, and yet, if we may credit report, it would seem as if there was already a British movement in this direction. Sometimes it is said that Great Britain desires to buy if Russia will sell. Sir George Simpson, governor-in-chief of the Hudson Bay Company, declared that without the strip on the coast underlet to the former by the Russian Company the interior would be "comparatively useless to England." Here, then, is a provocation to buy. Sometimes report assumes a graver character. A German scientific journal, in an elaborate paper entitled "The Russian Colonies on the Northwest Coast of America," after referring to the constant "pressure" upon Russia, proceeds to say that there are already crowds of adventurers from British Columbia and California now at the gold mines on the Stikine, which flows from British territory through the Russian possessions, who openly declare their purpose of driving the Russians out of this region. I refer to the *Archiv für Wissenschaftliche Kunde von Russland*, edited at Berlin as late as 1863, by A. Erman, vol. 22, pp. 47–70, and unquestionably the leading authority on Russian questions. At the same time it presents a curious passage bearing directly on British policy from the *British Colonist*, a newspaper of Victoria, on Vancouver's island. As this was regarded of sufficient importance to be translated into German for the instruction of the readers of a scientific journal, I shall be justified in laying it before you restored from the German to English. It is as follows:

"The information which we daily publish from the Stikine river very naturally excites public attention to a great extent. Whether the territory through which the river flows be considered in a political, commercial, or industrial light there is a probability that in a short time there will be a still more general interest in the claim. Not only will the intervention of the royal jurisdiction be demanded in order to give to it a complete form of government, but if the land proves to be as rich as there is now reason to believe it to be it is not improbable that it will result in negotiations between England and Russia for the transfer of the sea-coast to the British Crown. It certainly is not acceptable that a stream like the Stikine, which for one hundred and seventy to one hundred and ninety miles is navigable for steamers, which waters a territory so rich in gold that it will allure thousands of men—certainly it is not desirable that the business of such a highway should reach the interior through a Russian door of thirty miles of coast. The English population which occupies the interior cannot be so easily managed by the Russians as the Stikine Indians of the coast manage the Indians of the interior. Our business must be in British hands. Our resources, our energies, our undertakings cannot be fully developed in building up a Russian emporium at the mouth of the Stikine. We must have for our productions a depot over which the British flag waves. By the treaty of 1825 the navigation of the river is secured to us. The navigation of the Mississippi was also open to the United States before the Louisiana purchase, but the growing strength of the North made the attainment of that territory either by purchase or by might an evident necessity. We look upon the sea-coast of Stikine land in the same light. The strip of land which stretches along from Portland canal to Mount St. Elias with a breadth of thirty miles, and which according to the treaty of 1825 forms a part of Russian America, *must eventually become the property of Great Britain*, either as the direct result of the development of gold, or for reasons which are now yet in the beginning, but whose results are certain. For it is clearly undesirable that the strip three hundred miles long and thirty miles wide which is only used by the Russians for the collection of furs and walrus teeth shall forever control the entrance to our very extensive northern territory. It is a principle of England to acquire territory only as a point of defense. Canada, Nova Scotia, Malta, the Cape of Good Hope, and the great part of our Indian possessions were all acquired as defensive points. In Africa, India, and China the same rule is to-day followed by the Government. With a Power like Russia it would perhaps be more difficult to get ready, but if we need the sea-coast to help us in our business in the precious metals with the interior and for defense then we must have it. The United States needed Florida and Louisiana, and they took them. We need the shore of New Norfolk and New Cornwall.

"It is just as much the destiny of our Anglo-Norman race to possess the whole of Russian America, however wild and inhospitable it may be, as it has been the destiny of the Russian Northmen to prevail over northern Europe and Asia. As the wandering Jew and his phantom in the tale of Eugene Sue, so will the Anglo-Norman and the Russian yet look upon each other from the opposite side of Behring straits. Between the two races the northern half of the Old and New World must be divided. America must be ours.

"The present development of the precious metals in our hyperborean Eldorado will most probably hasten the annexation of the territory in question. It can hardly be doubted that the gold region of the Stikine extends away to the western source of the Mackenzie. In this case the increase of the business and of the population will exceed our most sanguine expectations. Who shall reap the profit of this? The mouths of rivers have as well before as since the time of railroads controlled the business of the interior. For our national pride the thought, however, is unbearable that the Russian eagle should possess a point which owes its importance to the British lion. The mouth of the Stikine must be ours, or at least an outer harbor must be established on British soil from which our steamers can pass the Russian girdle. Fort Simpson, Dundas Land, Portland canal, or some other convenient point, must be selected for this purpose. The necessity of speedy action in order to secure the control of the Stikine is apparent. If we let slip the opportunity, so shall we permit a Russian State to arrive at the door of a British colony."

Thus if we may credit this colonial ejaculation, caught up and preserved by German science, the Russian possessions were destined to round and complete the domain of Great Britain on this continent. The Russian "eagle" was to give way to the British "lion." The Anglo-Norman was to be master as far as Behring straits, across which he might survey his Russian neighbor. How this was to be accomplished is not precisely explained. The promises of gold on the Stikine failed, and it is not improbable that this colonial plan was as unsubstantial. Colonists become excited easily. This is not the first time in which Russian America has been menaced in a similar way. During the Crimean war there seemed to be in Canada a spirit not unlike that of the Vancouver journalist, unless we are misled by the able pamphlet of Mr. A. K. Roche, of Quebec, where, after describing Russian America as "richer in resources and capabilities than it has hitherto been allowed to be either by the English who shamefully gave it up, or by the Russians who cunningly obtained it," the author urges an expedition for its conquest and annexation. His proposition fell on the happy termination of the war, but it exists as a warning, with a notice also of a former English title, "shamefully" abandoned.

This region is distant enough from Great Britain; but there is an incident of past history which shows that distance from the metropolitan Government has not excluded the idea of war. Great Britain could hardly be more jealous of Russia on these coasts than was Spain in a former day, if we may credit the report of Humboldt. I quote again his authoritative work, *Essai Politique sur la Nouvelle Espagne*, (Tom. 1, page 345,) where it is recorded that as early as 1788, even while peace was still unbroken, the Spaniards could not bear the idea of Russians in this region, and when in 1790 the Emperor Paul declared war on Spain the hardy project was formed of an expedition from the Mexican ports of Monterey and San

Bias against the Russian colonies, on which the philosophic traveler remarks, in words which are recalled by the Vancouver manifesto, that "if this project had been executed the world would have witnessed two nations in conflict, which, occupying the opposite extremities of Europe, found themselves neighbors in another hemisphere on the eastern and western boundaries of their vast empires." Thus notwithstanding an intervening circuit of half the globe two great Powers were about to encounter each other on these coasts. But I hesitate to believe that the British of our day in any considerable numbers have adopted the early Spanish disquietude at the presence of Russia on this continent.

The Amity of Russia.

(5.) There is still another consideration concerning this Treaty which must not be disregarded. It attests and assures the amity of Russia. Even if you doubt the value of these possessions, the Treaty is a sign of friendship. It is a new expression of that *entente cordiale* between the two Powers which is a phenomenon of history. Though unlike in institutions, they are not unlike in recent experience. Sharers of a common glory in a great act of Emancipation, they also share together the opposition or antipathy of other nations. Perhaps this experience has not been without its effect in bringing them together. At all events, no coldness or unkindness has interfered at any time with their good relations. The archives of the State Department show an uninterrupted cordiality between the two Governments dating far back in our history. More than once Russia has offered her good offices between the United States and Great Britain; once also she was a recognized arbitrator. She offered her mediation to prevent war in 1812, and again by her mediation in 1815 brought about peace. Afterwards it was under her arbitration that questions with Great Britain arising under the treaty of Ghent were amicably settled in 1822. But it was during our recent troubles that we felt more than ever her friendly sentiments, although it is not improbable that the accident of position and of distance had its influence in preserving these undisturbed. The Rebellion, which tempted so many other Powers into its embrace, could not draw Russia from her habitual good will. Her solicitude for the Union was early declared. She made no unjustifiable concession of *ocean belligerency*, with all its immunities and powers, to rebels in arms against the Union. She furnished no hospitality to rebel cruisers; nor was any rebel agent ever received, entertained, or encouraged at St. Petersburg; while, on the other hand, there was an understanding that the United States should be at liberty to carry prizes into Russian ports. So natural and easy were the relations between the two Governments that such complaints as incidentally arose on either side were

amicably adjusted by verbal explanations without any written controversy. Positive acts occurred to strengthen these relations. As early as 1861 the two Governments came to an agreement to act together for the establishment of a connection between San Francisco and St. Petersburg by an interoceanic telegraph across Behring straits; and this agreement was subsequently sanctioned by Congress. Meanwhile occurred the visit of the Russian fleet in the winter of 1863, which was intended by the Emperor and accepted by the United States as a friendly demonstration. This was followed by a communication of the Secretary of State, dated 26th December, 1864, in the name of the President, inviting the Archduke Constantine to visit the United States, in which it was suggested that such a visit would be "beneficial to us and by no means unprofitable to Russia," but forbearing "to specify reasons," and assuring him that coming as a national guest he would receive a cordial and most demonstrative welcome. Affairs in Russia prevented the acceptance of this invitation. Afterwards, in the spring of 1866, Congress by solemn resolution declared the sympathies of the people of the United States with the Emperor on his escape from the madness of an assassin, and Mr. Fox, at the time Assistant Secretary of the Navy, was appointed to take the resolution of Congress to the Emperor, and, in discharge of this trust, to declare the friendly sentiments of our country for Russia. He was conveyed to Cronstadt in the monitor Miantonomah, the most formidable ship of our Navy; and thus this agent of war became a messenger of peace. The monitor and the minister were received in Russia with unbounded hospitality.

In relations such as I have described the cession of territory seems a natural transaction entirely in harmony with the past. It remains to hope that it may be a new link in an amity which, without effort, has overcome differences of institutions and intervening space on the globe.

SHALL THE TREATY BE RATIFIED?

Such are some of the obvious considerations of a general character bearing on the Treaty. The interests of the Pacific States; the extension of the national domain; the extension of republican institutions; the foreclosure of adverse British possessions and the amity of Russia; these are the points which we have passed in review. Most of these, if not all, are calculated to impress the public mind; but I can readily understand a difference of opinion with regard to the urgency of negotiation at this hour. Some may think that the purchase-money and the annual outlay which must follow might have been postponed for another decade, while Russia continued in possession as a trustee for our benefit. And yet some of the reasons for the Treaty do not seem to allow delay.

At all events, now that the Treaty has been

signed by plenipotentiaries on each side duly empowered, it is difficult to see how we can refuse to complete the purchase without putting to hazard the friendly relations which happily subsist between the United States and Russia. The overtures originally proceeded from us. After a delay of years, and other intervening propositions, the bargain was at length concluded. It is with nations as with individuals. A bargain once made must be kept. Even if still open to consideration it must not be lightly abandoned. I am satisfied that the dishonor of this Treaty, after what has passed, would be a serious responsibility for our country. As an international question, it would be tried by the public opinion of the world, and there are many, who, not appreciating the requirement of our Constitution by which a Treaty must have "the advice and consent of the Senate," would regard its rejection as bad faith. There would be jeers at us and jeers at Russia also; at us for levity in making overtures, and at Russia for levity in yielding to them. Had the Senate been consulted in advance, before the Treaty was signed or either Power publicly committed, as is often done on important occasions, it would now be under less constraint. On such a consultation there would have been an opportunity for all possible objections, and a large latitude to a reasonable discretion. Let me add that, while forbearing objection now, I hope that this Treaty may not be drawn into a precedent at least in the independent manner of its negotiation. I would save to the Senate an important power that justly belongs to it.

A CAVEAT.

But there is one other point on which I file my *caveat*. This Treaty must not be a precedent for a system of indiscriminate and costly annexation. Sincerely believing that republican institutions under the primacy of the United States must embrace this whole continent, I cannot adopt the sentiment of Jefferson, who while confessing satisfaction in settlements on the Pacific coast saw there in the future nothing but "free and independent Americans," bound to the United States only by "ties of blood and interest" without political unity. Nor am I willing to restrain myself to the principle so tersely expressed by Andrew Jackson in his letter to President Monroe, "Concentrate our population, confine our frontier to proper limits, until our country, to those limits, is filled with a dense population." But I cannot disguise my anxiety that every stage in our predestined future shall be by natural processes without war, and I would add even without purchase. There is no territorial aggrandizement which is worth the price of blood. Only under peculiar circumstances can it become the subject of pecuniary contract. Our triumph should be by growth and organic expansion in obedience to "preëstablished harmony," recognizing always the will of those who are to become our fellow-citizens. All this must be

easy if we are only true to ourselves. Our motto may be that of Goethe, "Without haste, without rest." Let the Republic be assured in tranquil liberty with all equal before the law and it will conquer by its sublime example. More happy than Austria, who acquired possessions by marriage, we shall acquire them by the attraction of republican institutions;

"Bella gerant alii: tu, felix Austria, nube:
Nam quæ Mars aliis, dat tibi regna Venus."

The famous epigram will be just as applicable to us, inasmuch as our acquisitions will be under the sanction of wedlock to the Republic. There may be wedlock of a people as well as of a prince. Meanwhile our first care should be to improve and elevate the Republic, whose sway will be so comprehensive. Plant it with schools; cover it with churches; fill it with libraries; make it abundant with comfort so that poverty shall disappear; keep it constant in the assertion of Human Rights. And here we may fitly recall those words of antiquity, which Cicero quoted from the Greek, and which Webster in our day quoted from Cicero, "You have a Sparta; adorn it."

SOURCES OF INFORMATION UPON RUSSIAN AMERICA.

I am now brought to consider the character of these possessions and their probable value. Here I am obliged to confess a dearth of authentic information easily accessible. There are few among us who read Russian, so that works in this language are locked up from the world. One of these, in two large and showy volumes, is now before me, entitled "A Historical Survey of the Formation of the Russian-American Company, and its progress to the present time, by P. Teshmenew, St. Petersburg." The first volume appeared in 1860, and the second in 1863. Here, among other things, is a tempting engraving of Sitka, wrapped in mists, with the sea before and the snow-capped mountains darkened with forest behind. Judging from the table of contents, which has been translated for me by a Russian, the book ought to be instructive. There is also another Russian work of an official character, which appeared in 1861 at St. Petersburg in the *Morskoi Sbornich*, or Naval Review, and is entitled "Materials for the History of the Russian Colonies on the Coasts of the Pacific." The report of Captain Lieutenant Golowin made to the Grand Duke Constantine in 1861, with which we have become acquainted through a scientific German journal, appeared originally in the same review. These are recent productions. After the early voyages of Behring, first ordered by Peter the Great and supervised by the Imperial Academy at St. Petersburg, the spirit of geographical research seems to have subsided at St. Petersburg. Other enterprises absorbed the attention. And yet I would not do injustice to the voyages of Billings, recounted by Sauer, or of Lisiansky, Krusenstern, and Langsdorf, or of Kotzebue, all under the auspices of Russia, the last of which may compare with any as a contribution to science. I may add Lütke also; but Kotzebue was a worthy successor to Behring and Cook.

Beside these official contributions, most of which are by no means fresh, there are materials derived from casual navigators, who, scudding these seas, rested in the harbors there as the water-fowl on its flight; from whalemen, who were there merely as Nimrods of the ocean; or from adventurers in quest of the rich furs which it furnished. There are also the gazetteers and geographies; but they are less instructive on this head than usual, being founded on information now many years old.

Perhaps no region of equal extent on the globe, unless we except the interior of Africa or possibly Greenland, is as little known. Here I do not speak for myself alone. A learned German, whom I have already quoted, after saying that the explorations have been limited to the coast, testifies that "the interior, not only of the continent, but even of the island of Sitka, is to-day unexplored, and is in every respect *terra incognita*." The same has been repeated of the islands also. Admiral Lütke, whose circumnavigation of the globe began in 1825, and whose work bears date in 1835, says of the Aleutian archipelago, that "although frequented for more than a century by Russian vessels and those of other nations it is to-day almost as little known as in the time of Cook." Another writer of authority, the compiler of the official work on the People of Russia, published as late as 1862, speaks of the interior as "a mystery." And yet another says that our ignorance with regard to this region would make it a proper scene for a chapter of Gulliver's Travels.

Where so little was known there was scope for invention. Imagination was made to supply the place of knowledge, and poetry pictured the savage desolation in much-admired verse. Campbell, in the Pleasures of Hope, while exploring "earth's loneliest bounds and ocean's wildest shore," reaches this region, which he portrays:

"Lo! to the wintry winds the pilot yields,
His bark careering o'er unfathomed fields.
Now far he sweeps, where scarce a summer smiles,
On Behring's rocks, or Greenland's naked isles;
Cold in his midnight watch the breezes blow,
From wastes that slumber in eternal snow,
And waft across the wave's tumultuous roar
The wolf's long howl from Ounalaska's shore."

All of which, so far at least as it describes this region, is inconsistent with the truth. The poet ignores the isothermal line, which plays such a conspicuous part on the Pacific coast. Here the evidence is positive. Portlock, the navigator, who was there toward the close of the last century, after describing Cook's inlet, which is several degrees north of Ounalaska, records his belief "that the climate here is not so severe as has been generally supposed; for in the course of traffic with the natives they frequently brought berries of several sorts, and in particular blackberries equally fine with those met with in England." (Voyage, p. 118.) Kotzebue, who was here later, records that he found the weather "pretty warm at Ounalaska." (Voyage, vol. 1, p. 275.) South of the Aleutians the climate is warmer still. The poet ignores natural history also as regards the distribution of animals. Curiously enough, it does not appear that there are "wolves" on any of the Aleutians. Coxe, in his work on Russian Discoveries, (p. 174,) records that "reindeer, bears, *wolves*, and ice-foxes are not to be found on these islands." But he was never there. Meares, who was in those seas, says "the *only animals* on these islands are foxes, some of which are black." (Voyage, vol. 1, p. 16.) Cook, who was at Ounalaska twice, and once made a prolonged stay, expressly says, "Foxes and weasels were the *only quadrupeds* we saw; they told us that they had hares also." (Voyage, vol. 2, p. 518.) But quadrupeds like these hardly sustain the exciting picture. The same experienced navigator furnishes a glimpse of the inhabitants as they appeared to him, which would make us tremble if the "wolves" of the poet were numerous. He says that "to all appearance they are the most peaceable, inoffensive people he ever met with;" and Cook had been at Otaheite. "No such thing as an offensive or defensive weapon was seen amongst the natives of Ounalaska." (*Ibid.*, pp. 509, 515.) Then at least the inhabitants did not share the ferocity of the "wolves" and of the climate. Another navigator fascinates us by a description of the boats of Ounalaska, which struck him "with amazement beyond expression;" and he goes on to say, "If perfect symmetry, smoothness, and proportion constitute beauty, they are beautiful beyond anything that I ever beheld. I have seen some of them as transparent as oiled paper." (Billings's Voyages, p. 15.) But these are the very boats that buffet "the wave's tumultuous roar," while "the breezes" waft the "wolf's long howl." This same navigator introduces another feature. According to him the Russians sojourning there "seem to have no desire to leave this place, where they enjoy that indolence so pleasing to their minds." (P. 161.) The lotus eaters of Homer were no better off. The picture is completed by another touch from Lütke. Admitting the want of trees on the island, the admiral suggests that their place is supplied not only by luxuriant grass, but by wood thrown upon the coast, including trunks of camphor from Chinese and Japanese waters, and "a tree which gives forth the odor of the rose." (Voyage, Tom. 1, p. 132.) Such is a small portion of the testimony, most of which was in print before the poet wrote.

Nothing has been written about this region, whether the coast or the islands, more authentic or interesting than the narrative of Captain Cook on his third and last voyage. He saw with intelligence, and described with clearness almost elegant. The record of Captain Portlock's voyage from London to the northwest coast in 1786, 1787, and 1788 seems to be honest, and is instructive. Captain Meares, whose voyage was contemporaneous, saw and exposed the importance of trade between the northwest coast and China. Vancouver, who came a little later, has described some parts of this coast. La Pérouse, the unfortunate French navigator, has afforded another picture of the coast painted with French colors. Before him was La Maurelle, a Frenchman sailing in the service of Spain, who was on the coast in 1775, a portion of whose journal is preserved in the appendix to the volumes of La Pérouse. After him was Marchand, also a Frenchman, who, during a voyage round the world, stopped here in 1791. The voyage of the latter, published in three quartos, is accompanied by an Historical Introduction, which is a mine of information on all the voyages to this coast. Then came the several successive Russian voyages already mentioned. Later came the *Voyage round the world* by Captain Belcher, with a familiar sketch of life at Sitka, where he stopped in 1837, and an engraving representing the arsenal and light-house there. Then came the *Journey round the world* in 1841 and 1842 by Sir George Simpson, governor-in-chief of the Hudson Bay Company, containing an account of a visit to Sitka and the hospitality of its governor. To these I may add *The Nautical Magazine* for 1849, volume 18, which contains a few excellent pages about Sitka; the *Journal of the London Geographical Society* for 1841, volume 11, and for 1852, volume 12, where this region is treated under the head of Arctic languages and animal life; Burney's *Russian and Northeastern Voyages*; the magnificent work entitled *Les Peuples de la Russie*, which appeared at St. Petersburg in 1862, on the tenth centennial anniversary of the foundation of the Russian empire, a copy of which is in the Astor Library; the very recent work of Murray on the *Geographical Distribution of Mammals;* the work of Sir John Richardson, *Fauna Boreali-Americana;* *Latham on Nationalities* in the chapters which treat of the population of Russian America; the *Encyclopedia Britannica;* and the admirable *Atlas of Physical Geography* by Keith Johnston. I mention also an elaborate article by Holmberg, in the Transactions of the Finland Society of Sciences at Helsingfors, said to be replete with information on the Ethnography of the Northwest Coast.

Perhaps the most precise and valuable information has been contributed by Germany. The Germans are the best of geographers; besides many Russian contributions are in German. Müller, who recorded the discoveries of Behring, was a German. Nothing more important on this subject has ever appeared than the German work of the Russian Admiral Von Wrangel, *Statistische und Ethnographische Nachrichten über die Russichen Besitzungen an der Nordwestküste von America,*

first published by Baer in his Russian *Beiträge* in 1839. There is also the *Verhandlungen der Russisch-Kaiserlichen Mineralogischen Gessellschaft zu St. Petersburg,* 1848 and 1849, which contains an elaborate article, in itself a volume, on the orography and geology of the northwest coast and the adjoining islands, at the end of which is a bibliographical list of the works and materials illustrating the discovery and history of the west half of North America and the neighboring seas. I may also refer generally to the *Archiv für Wissenschaftliche Kunde von Russland,* edited by Erman, but especially the volume for 1863, containing the abstract of Golowin's report on the Russian Colonies in North America as it appeared originally in the *Morskoi Sbornich.* Besides these there are Wappäus *Handbuch von Geographie und Statistik von Nord Amerika,* published at Leipsic in 1855; Peterman in his *Mittheilungen über wichtige neue Erforschungen auf dem gesammtgebiete der Geographie* for 1856, vol. 2, p. 486; for 1859, vol. 5, p. 41; and for 1863, vol. 9, pp. 70, 236, 277, 278; Kittlitz *Denkwürdigkeiten einer Reise nach dem Russischen America durch Kamtschatka,* published at Gotha in 1858; also by the same author *The Vegetation of the Coasts and Islands of the Pacific* translated from the German and published at London in 1861.

Much recent information has been derived from the great companies possessing the monopoly of trade here. Latterly there has been an unexpected purveyor in the Russian American Telegraph Company, under the direction of Colonel Charles L. Bulkley, and here our own countrymen come to help us. To this expedition we are indebted for authentic evidence with regard to the character of the country and the great rivers which traverse it. The Smithsonian Institution and the Chicago Academy of Sciences coöperated with the Telegraph Company in the investigation of the Natural History of the region. Major Kennicott, a young naturalist, originally in the service of the Institution, and Director of the Museum of the Chicago Academy, was the enterprising chief of the Youkon division of the expedition. While in the midst of his valuable labors he died suddenly in the month of May last at Nulato, on the banks of the great river, the Kwichpak, which may be called the Mississippi of the North, far away in the interior and on the confines of the Arctic Circle, where the sun was visible all night. Even after death he was still an explorer. From this remote outpost his remains, after descending the unknown river in an Esquimaux boat of seal skins, steered by the faithful companion of his labors, were transported by way of Panama to his home at Chicago, where he now lies buried. Such an incident cannot be forgotten, and his name will always remind us of courageous enterprise, before which distance and difficulty disappeared. He was not a beginner when he entered into the service of the Telegraph Company. Already he had visited the Youkon country by the way of the Mackenzie river, and contributed to the Smithsonian Institution important information with regard to its geography and natural history, some of which will be found in their reports. Nature in novel forms was open to him. The birds here maintained their kingdom. All about him was the mysterious breeding-place of the canvas-back duck, whose eggs, never before seen by a naturalist, covered acres.

If we look to maps for information, here again we find ourselves disappointed. Latterly the coast is outlined and described with reasonable completeness; so also are the islands. This is the contribution of navigators and of recent Russian charts. But the interior is little more than a blank, calling to mind "the pathless downs," where, according to Prior, the old geographers "place elephants instead of towns." I have already referred to what purports to be a "General Map of the Russian Empire," published by the Academy of Sciences at St. Petersburg in 1776, and republished at London in 1787, where Russian America does not appear. I might mention also that Captain Cook complained in his day of the Russian maps as "wonderfully erroneous." On his return English maps recorded his explorations and the names he assigned to different parts of the coast. These were reproduced in St. Petersburg, and the Russian copy was then reproduced in London, so that geographical knowledge was very little advanced. Some of the best maps of this region are by Germans, who always excel in maps. Here, for instance, is an excellent map of the Aleutian islands and the neighboring coasts, especially to illustrate their orography and geography, which will be found at the end of the volume of *Transactions of the Imperial Mineralogical Society* at St. Petersburg, to which I have already referred.

Late maps attest the tardiness of information. Here, for instance, is an excellent map of North America, purporting to be published by the Geographical Institute of Weimar as late as 1859, on which we have the Youkon pictured, very much like the Niger in Africa, as a large river meandering in the interior without any outlet to the sea. Here also is a Russian map of this very region, as late as 1861, in which the course of the Youkon is left in doubt. On other maps, as in the Atlas of Keith Johnston, it is pictured under another name as entering into the Frozen ocean. But the secret is penetrated at last. Recent discovery by the enterprise of our citizens in the service of the Telegraph Company fixes that this river is an affluent of the Kwichpak, as the Missouri is an affluent of the Mississippi, and enters into Behring sea, by many mouths, between the parallels of 64° and 65°. After the death of Major Kennicott a division of his party, with nothing but a skin boat, ascended the river to Fort Youkon, where it bifurcates, and descended it again to Nulato, thus establishing the entire course from its sources in the Rocky mountains for a distance exceeding a thousand miles. I have before me now an outline map just prepared by our *Coast Survey*, where this correction is made. But this is only the harbinger of the maturer labors of our accomplished bureau when the coasts of this region are under the jurisdiction of the United States.

In closing this abstract of authorities, being the chief sources of original information on this subject, I cannot forbear expressing my satisfaction that, with the exception of a single work, all these may be found in the Congressional Library, now so happily enriched by the rare collection of the Smithsonian Institution. Sometimes individuals are like libraries; and this seems to be illustrated in the case of Professor Baird, of the Smithsonian Institution, who is thoroughly informed on all questions connected with the Natural History of Russian America, and also of George Gibbs, Esq., now of Washington, who is the depositary of valuable knowledge, the result of his own personal studies and observations, with regard to the native races.

CHARACTER AND VALUE OF RUSSIAN AMERICA.

I pass now to a consideration of the character and value of these possessions, as seen under these different heads: *first*, government; *secondly*, population; *thirdly*, climate; *fourthly*, vegetable products; *fifthly*, mineral products; *sixthly*, furs; and *seventhly*, fisheries. Of these I shall speak briefly in their order. There are certain words of a general character, which I introduce by way of preface. I quote from Blodgett on the *Climatology of the United States and of the temperate Latitudes of the North American continent* :

"It is most surprising that so little is known of the great islands and the long line of coast from Puget's sound to Sitka, ample as its resources must be even for recruiting the transient commerce of the Pacific, independent of its immense intrinsic value. To the region bordering the northern Pacific the finest maritime positions belong throughout its entire extent; and no part of the west of Europe exceeds it in the advantages of equable climate, fertile soil, and commercial accessibility of the coast. The western slope of the Rocky mountain system may be included as a part of this maritime region, embracing an immense area from the forty-fifth to the sixtieth parallel and five degrees of longitude in width. The cultivable service of this district cannot be much less than three hundred thousand square miles."

From this sketch, which is in the nature of a picture, I pass to the different heads.

Government.

I. The Russian settlements were for a long time without any regular *Government*. They were little more than temporary lodgments for purposes of trade, where the will of the stronger prevailed. The natives, who had enslaved each other, became in turn the slaves of these mercenary adventurers. Captain Cook records "the great subjection" of the natives at Oonalaska when he was there in

1778, and a Russian navigator, twenty years later, describes the islands generally as "under the sway of roving hunters more savage than any tribes he had hitherto met with." (Billings's Voyage, p. 274.) At Ounalaska the Russians for a long time employed all the men in the chase, "taking the fruits of their labor to themselves."

The first trace of government which I find was in 1790, at the important island of Kodiak, or the Great Island, as it was called, where a Russian company was established under the direction of a Greek by the name of Delareff, who, according to the partial report of a Russian navigator, "governed with the strictest justice, as well natives as Russians, and established a school, where the young natives were taught the Russian language, reading. and writing." (Billings, p. 171.) Here were about fifty Russians, including officers of the company, and another person described as there "on the part of Government to collect tribute." The establishment consisted of five houses after the Russian fashion; barracks laid out on either side somewhat like the boxes at a coffee-house, with different offices, which are represented as follows: "An office of appeal to settle disputes, levy fines, and punish offenders by a regular trial; here Delareff presides; and I believe that few courts of justice pass a sentence with more impartiality; an office of receival and delivery, both for the company and for tribute; the commissary's department; counting-house; all in this building, at one end of which is Delareff's habitation." (Ibid., p. 173.) If this picture is not overdrawn, and it surely is, affairs here did not improve with time.

It seems that there were various small companies, of which that at Kodiak was the most considerable, all of which were finally fused into one large Trading Company, known as the Russian American Company, which was organized in 1799, under a charter from the Emperor Paul, with the power of administration throughout the whole region, including the coasts and the islands. In this respect it was not unlike the East India Company, which has played such a part in English history; but it may be more properly compared to the Hudson Bay Company, of which it was a Russian counterpart. The charter was for a term of years, but it has been from time to time extended, and, as I understand, is now on the point of expiring. The powers of the company are sententiously described by the *Almanach de Gotha* for 1867, where, under the head of Russia, it says that "to the present time Russian America has been the *property of a company.*"

I know no limitation upon the company, except that latterly it has been bound to appoint its chief functionary, called "Administrator General," from the higher officers of the Imperial navy, when he becomes invested with what are declared the prerogatives of a governor in Siberia. This requirement has doubtless secured the superior order of magistrates which the country has latterly enjoyed. Among these have been Baron Wrangel, an admiral, who was there at the time of the treaty with Great Britain in 1825; Captain Koupreanoff, who had commanded the Azof, a ship of the line, in the Black sea, and spoke English well; Captain Etholine; Admiral Fujurelm, who, after being there five years, was made governor of the province of the Amoor; Admiral Wodski and Prince Macksoutoff, an admiral also, who is the present Administrator General. The term of service is ordinarily five years.

The seat of government is the town of New Archangel, better known by its aboriginal name of Sitka, with a harbor as smooth and safe as a pond. Its present population cannot be far from one thousand souls, although even this is changeable. In the spring, when sailors leave for the sea and trappers for the chase, it has been reduced to as few as one hundred and eighty. It was not without a question that Sitka at last prevailed as the metropolis. Lütke sets forth reasons elaborately urged in favor of St. Paul on the island of Kodiak. (Voyage, Tom. 1, p. 153.)

The first settlement there was in 1800 by Baranow, the superintendent of the company, whose life was passed in this country, and whose name has been given to the island. But the settlement made slow progress. Lisiansky, who was there in 1804, records that "from his entrance into Sitka sound there was not to be seen on the shore the least vestige of habitation." (P. 145.) The natives had set themselves against a settlement there. Meanwhile the seat of government was at Kodiak, of which we have an early and friendly glimpse. I quote what Lisiansky says, as exhibiting in a favorable light the beginning of that government which has been transferred to the United States:

"The island of Kodiak, with the rest of the Russian settlements along the northwest coast of America, are superintended by a kind of governor general or commander-in-chief, who has agents under him, appointed, like himself, by the company at Petersburg. The smaller settlements have each a Russian overseer. These overseers are chosen by the governor, and are selected for the office in consequence of their long services and orderly conduct. They have the power of punishing, to a certain extent, those whom they superintend; but are themselves amenable to the governor if they abuse their power by acts of injustice. The seat of government is on the harbor of St. Paul, which has a barrack, different storehouses, several respectable wooden habitations, and a church, the only one to be found on the coast."—*Ibid.*, p. 214.

From this time the company seems to have established itself on the coast. Lisiansky speaks of "a single hunting party of nine hundred men, gathered from different places, as Alaska, Kodiak, Kenay, Cook's inlet, and commanded by thirty-six *toyons*, who are subordinate to the Russians in the service of them American company, and receive from them their orders." (*Ibid.*, 153.) From another source I learn that the inhabitants of Kodiak and of the Aleutian islands were regarded as "immediate subjects of the company;" the males from eighteen to fifty being bound to serve it for the term of three years each. They were employed in the chase. The population of Alaska and of the two great bays, Cook's inlet and Prince William sound, were also subject to the company; but they were held to a yearly tax in furs without any regular service, and they could trade only with the company. Otherwise they were independent. This seems to have been before the division of the whole into districts, all under the company, which, though primarily for the business of the company. may be regarded as so many distinct jurisdictions, each with local powers of government.

Among these were two districts which I mention only to put aside, as not included in the present cession: (1.) The *Kurile Islands*, being the group nestling near the coast of Japan, on the Asiatic side of the dividing line between the two continents. (2.) The *Ross* settlement in California, now abandoned.

There remain five other districts: (1.) The *District of Atcha*, with the bureau at this island, embracing the two western groups of the Aleutians known as the Andreanowsky islands and the Rat islands; and also the group about Behring's island, which is not embraced in the present cession. (2.) The *District of Ouna-lashka*, with the bureau at this island, embracing the Fox islands, the peninsula of Alaska to the meridian of the Shumagin islands, including these and also the Prybelov islands to the north of the peninsula. (3.) The *District of Kodiak*, embracing the peninsula of Alaska east of the meridian of the Shumagin islands, and the coast westward to Mount St. Elias, with the adjacent islands, including Kodiak, Cook's inlet, and Prince William sound; then northward along the coast of Bristol bay, and the country watered by the Nushagak and Kuskokwim rivers; all of which is governed from Kodiak with redoubts or palisaded stations at Nushagak, Cook's inlet, and Prince William sound. (4.) The *Northern District*, embracing the country of the Kwichpak and of Norton's sound, under the direction of the commander of the redoubt at St. Michaels; leaving the country northward, with the islands St. Lawrence and St. Mathews, not embraced in this district, but visited direct from Sitka. (5.) The *District of Sitka*, embracing the coast from Mount St. Elias, where the Kodiak district ends, southward to the latitude of 54° 40′, with the adjacent islands. But this district has been curtailed by a lease of the Russian American Company in 1839, for the space of ten years, and subsequently renewed, in which this company, in consideration of the annual payment of two thousand otter skins of Columbia river, underlets to the Hudson Bay Company all its franchise for the strip of continent between Cape

Spencer at the north and the latitude of 54° 40′, excluding the adjacent islands.

The central government of all these districts is at Sitka, from which emanates all orders and instructions. Here also is the chief factory, from which supplies are forwarded to different places, and where the proceeds of the trade are collected.

The operations of the Government may be seen in its receipts and expenditures, including its salaries and allowances. In the absence of a complete series of such statistics to the present time, I mass together what I have been able to glean in different fields, relating to particular years, knowing well its unsatisfactory character. But each item has its instruction for us.

The capital of the company, in buildings, wares, and vessels, in 1833, was said to be 3,658,577 rubles. In 1838 the company possessed twelve vessels, amounting together to fifteen hundred and fifty-six tons, most of which were built at Sitka. According to Wappäus, who follows Wrangel, the salaries of the officers and workmen of the company in 1832 amounted to 442,877 rubles. At that time the persons in its service numbered 1,025, of whom 556 were Russians, 152 Creoles, and 317 Aleutians. In 1851 there were in the service of the company 1 staff officer, 3 officers of the Imperial navy, 1 officer of engineers, 4 civil officers, 30 religious officers, and 686 servants. The expenses of the company from 1826 to 1833, a period of seven years, were 6,608,077 rubles. These become interesting to us when it is considered that, besides what was paid on account of furs, and the support of the persons in the service of the company, were other items incident to government, such as ship-building, navigation, fortifications, hospitals, schools, and churches. From a later authority it appears that the receipts of the company, reported at St. Petersburg for the year 1855, was 832,749 rubles, against expenses, 683,892 rubles, incurred for "administration in Russia and the colonies," insurance, transportation, and duties. The relative proportion of these different expenses does not appear. I have another report for 1857, where the revenue was 832,749 rubles, with expenditures of 683,892 rubles, leaving the difference for dividends, which were fixed at 18 rubles a share.

These are explained by other statistics, which I am able to give from the report of Golowin, who furnishes the receipts and expenditures of the company from 1850 to 1859, inclusive. The silver ruble, which is the money employed in the table, is taken at our Mint for seventy-five cents.

Receipts from 1850 to 1859, inclusive.

	Silver roubles.
Tea traffic	4,145,863.79
Sale of furs	1,709,149
Commercial licenses	2,463,285.61
Other traffics	170,253.76
Total	8,528,551.13

Expenditures from 1850 to 1859, inclusive.	
	Silver roubles.
Sustenance of the colony	2,288,207.20
Colonies churches	71,723.18
Benevolent institutions	143,366.23
Principal administrative officers	1,536,436.49
Tea duty	1,764,559.85
Transportation and packing of tea	586,901.72
Purchase and transportation of merchandise	213,696.29
Insurance of tea and merchandise	217,026.55
Loss during war and by shipwreck	132,820.20
Reconstruction of the company's house in St. Petersburg	76,976
Capital for the use of the poor	6,773.02
Revenue fund capital	135,460.40
Dividends	1,354,604
Total	8,528,551.13

Analyzing this table we shall arrive at a clearer insight into the affairs of the company. If its receipts have been considerable they have been subject to serious deductions. From the expenditures we may also learn something of the obligations which we are about to assume.

From another table I learn that during this same period 122,006 rubles were received for ice, mostly sent to California; 26,399 rubles for timber, and 6,250 rubles for coal. I think it not improbable that these items are included in the list of "receipts" under the term "other traffics."

In Russia the churches belong to the Government, and this rule prevails in these districts. where there are four Greek churches and five Greek chapels. There is also a Protestant church at Sitka. I am glad to add that at the latter place there is a public library, which some years ago contained seventeen hundred volumes, together with journals, maps, atlases, and mathematical instruments. In Atcha, Oanalaska, Kodiak, and Sitka schools are said to have been maintained at the expense of the company, though not on a very comprehensive scale; for Admiral Wrangel mentions only ninety boys as enjoying these advantages in 1839. In Ounalaska and Kodiak there were at the same time orphan asylums for girls, where there were in all about thirty. But the admiral adds that "these useful institutions will, without doubt, be improved to the utmost." Besides these, which are confined to particular localities, there is said to be a hospital near every factory in all the districts.

I have no means of knowing if these territorial subdivisions have undergone any recent modifications. They will be found in the Russichen Besitzungen of Wrangel, published in 1839; in the Geographie of Wappäus in 1856, and in the Archiv von Russland of 1863, containing the article on the report of Golowin. I am thus particular with regard to them from a double motive. Besides helping to an understanding of the existing government they may afford suggestions of practical importance in any future organization.

The company has not been without criticism. Some of the pictures of it are by no means rose color. These, too, may furnish instruction for the future. Early in the century its administration was the occasion of open and repeated complaint. It was pronounced harsh and despotic. Langsdorf is indignant that "a free-trading company should exist independent of the Government, not confined within any definite regulations, but who can exercise their authority free and uncontrolled, nay, even unpunished, over so vast an extent of country." In stating the case he adds that "the Russian subject here enjoys no protection of his property, lives in no security, and if oppressed has no one to whom he can apply for justice. The agents of the factories and their subordinates, influenced by humor or interest, decide everything arbitrarily." (Voyages, vol. 2, p. 70.) And this arbitrary power seemed to prevail wherever a factory was established: "the stewardship in each single establishment is entirely despotic; though nominally depending upon the principal factory these stewards do just what they please, without the possibility of being called to account." (Ibid., vol. 2, p. 69.) If such was the condition of Russians, what must have been that of the natives? Here the witness answers: "I have seen the Russian fur-hunters dispose of the lives of the natives solely according to their own arbitrary will, and put these defenseless creatures to death in the most horrible manner." (P. 70.) Krusenstern concurs in this testimony, and, if possible, darkens the colors. According to him "every one must obey the iron rule of the agent of the American company; nor can there be either personal property or individual security where there are no laws. The chief agent of the American company is the boundless despot over an extent of country which, comprising the Aleutian islands, stretches from 57° to 60° of latitude and from 130° to 190° of east longitude;" and he adds, in a note, "there are no courts of justice in Kodiak, nor any of the company's possessions." (Voyages, vol. 2, p. 107.) Kotzebue, who came later, while confessing his incompetency to speak on the treatment of the natives by the company, declares his "wounded feelings and commiseration." (Voyage, vol. 3, p. 314.) It is too probable that the melancholy story of our own aborigines has been repeated here. As these criticisms were by Russian officers they must have had a certain effect. I cannot believe that the recent government, administered by the enlightened magistrates of whom we have heard, has been obnoxious to such terrible accusations; nor must it be forgotten that the report of Lisiansky, the other Russian officer, who was there at the same time. is much less painful.

Baranow, who had been so long superintendent, retired in 1818. He is praised much by Langsdorf, who saw him in 1806, and by Lütke, who was at Sitka in 1828. Both attribute to him a genius for his place and a disinterested devotion to the interests of the company, whose confidence he enjoyed to the end. Although administering affairs here for more than a generation without rendering any accounts, he died poor. He was succeeded by Captain Haguemeister. Since then, according to Lütke, an infinity of reforms has taken place by which order and system have been introduced into the government.

The Russian officer, Captain Golowin, who visited these possessions in 1860, has recommended certain institutional reforms, which are not without interest to us at this time. His recommendations concern the governor and the people. According to him the governor should be appointed by the Crown with the concurrence of the company, removable only when his continuance is plainly injurious to the colony; he should be subject only to the Crown, and his powers should be limited, especially in regard to the natives; he should provide protection for the colonists by means of cruisers, and should personally visit every district annually; the colonists, creoles, and subject natives, such as the Aleutians, should be governed by magistrates of their own selection; the name of "free creole" should cease; all disputes should be settled by the local magistrates unless the parties desire an appeal to the governor; schools should be encouraged, and, if necessary, provided at the public expense. Surely these suggestions, which are in the nature of a Reform Bill, foreshadow a condition of self-government in harmony with republican institutions.

It is evident that these Russian settlements, distributed through an immense region and far from any civilized neighborhood, have little in common with those of European nations elsewhere, unless we except those of Denmark on the west coast of Greenland. Nearly all are on the coast or the islands. They are nothing but "villages" or "factories," under the protection of palisades. Sitka is an exception, due unquestionably to its selection as the headquarters of the government, and also to the eminent character of the governors who have made it their home. The Executive Mansion and the social life there have been described by recent visitors, who acknowledged the charms of politeness on this distant northwestern coast. Lütke describes life among its fogs, and especially the attractions of the governor's house. This was in the time of Admiral Wrangel, whose wife, possessing a high education, embellished this wilderness by her presence, and exhibited the example of a refined and happy household. His account of Sitkan hospitality differs in some respects from that of the English writers who succeeded. He records that fish was the staple dish at the tables of functionaries as well as of the poor, and that the chief functionary himself was rarely able to have meat for dinner. During the winter a species of wild sheep, the Musimon or Argalis, also known in Siberia and hunted in the forests, furnished an occasional supply. But a fish diet did not prevent his house from being delightful.

Sir Edward Belcher, the English circumnavigator, while on his voyage round the world, stopped there. From him we have an account of the Executive Mansion and fortifications, which will not be out of place in this attempt to portray the existing government. The house is of wood, described as "solid," one hundred and forty feet in length by seventy feet wide, of two stories, with lofts, capped by a light-house in the center of the roof which is covered with sheet iron. It is about sixty feet above the sea level, and completely commands all the anchorages in the neighborhood. Behind is a line of picketed logs twenty-five feet in height, flanked at the angles by blockhouses, loop-holed and furnished with small guns and swivels. The fortifications when complete "will comprise five sides, upon which forty pieces of cannon will be mounted, principally old ship guns, varying from twelve to twenty-four pounders." The arsenal is praised for the best of cordage in ample stores and for the best of artificers in every department. The interior of the Greek church was found to be "splendid, quite beyond conception in such a place as this." The school and hospital had "a comparative cleanliness and much to admire, although a man-of-war's man's ideas of cleanliness are occasionally acute." But it is the social life which seems to have most surprised the gallant captain. After telling us that "on Sunday all the officers, civil and military, dine at the governor's," he introduces us to an evening party and dance, which the latter gave to show his English guest "the female society of Sitka," and records that everything "passed delightfully," especially that "the ladies, although self-taught, acquitted themselves with all the ease and elegance communicated by European instruction." Sir Edward adds that "the society is indebted principally to the governor's elegant and accomplished lady, who is of one of the first Russian families, for much of this polish." And he describes sympathetically her long journey through Siberia with her husband, "on horseback or mules, enduring great hardships in a most critical moment, in order to share with him the privations of this barbarous region." But according to him barbarism is disappearing; and he concludes by declaring that "the whole establishment appears to be rapidly on the advance, and at no distant period we may hear of a trip to Norfolk sound through America as little more than a summer excursion." (Belcher's Voyage, vol. 1, p. 107.) Is not this time near at hand?

Shortly afterwards, Sir George Simpson, governor-in-chief of the Hudson Bay Company, on his overland journey round the world, stopped at Sitka. He had just crossed the continent by way of the Red river settlements to Vancouver. He, too, seems to have been pleased. He shows us in the harbor "five sailing vessels, ranging between two hundred and three hundred and fifty tons, besides a large bark in the offing in tow of a steamer," and he carries us to the Executive Mansion, already described, which reappears as "a suite of apartments, communicating, according to the Russian fashion, with each other, all of the public rooms being handsomely decorated and richly furnished; commanding a view of the whole establishment, which was in fact a little village, while about half way down the rock two batteries on terraces frowned respectively over land and water." There was another Administrator General since the visit of Sir Edward Belcher; but again the wife plays her charming part. After portraying her as a native of Helsingfors, in Finland, the visitor adds, "So this pretty and lady-like woman had come to this secluded home from the farthest extremity of the empire." Evidently in a mood beyond contentment, he says, "We sat down to a good dinner in the French style, the party, in addition to our host and hostess and ourselves, comprising twelve of the company's officers;" and his final judgment seems to be given when he says, "The good folks appear to live well. The surrounding country abounds in the chevreuil, [roebuck,] the finest meat that I ever ate, with the single exception of moose, while in a little stream within a mile of the fort salmon are so plentiful that, when ascending the river, they have been known literally to embarrass the movements of a canoe." (Simpson's Journey, vol. 1, page 227.) Such is the testimony. With these concluding pictures I turn from the government.

Population.

II. I come now to the *Population*, which may be considered in its numbers and in its character. In neither respect, perhaps, can it add much to the value of the country, except so far as native hunters and trappers are needed for the supply of furs. Professor Agassiz touches this point in a letter which I have just received from him, where he says: "To me the fact that there is as yet hardly any population would have great weight, as this secures the settlement to our race." But we ought to know something at least of the people about to become the subjects of our jurisdiction, if not our fellow-citizens.

First. In trying to arrive at an idea of their *numbers*, I begin with Lippincott's Gazetteer, as it is the most accessible, according to which the whole population in 1855, aboriginal, Russian, and Creole, was 61,000. The same estimate appears also in the London Imperial Gazetteer and in the *Geographie* of Wappäus. Keith Johnston, in his Atlas, calls the population in 1852, 66,000. McCulloch, in the last edition of his Geographical Dictionary, puts it as high as 72,375. On the other hand, the *Almanach de Gotha* for the present year, received only a few weeks ago, calls it in round numbers 50,000. This estimate seems to have been adopted substantially from the great work entitled *Les Peuples de la Russie*, which from

its character I am disposed to consider as the best authority.

Exaggerations are common with regard to the inhabitants of newly-acquired possessions, and this distant region has been no exception. An enthusiastic estimate once placed its population as high as four hundred thousand. Long ago Schelekoff, an early Russian adventurer, reported that he had subjected to the Crown of Russia fifty thousand "men" in the island of Kodiak alone. But Lisiansky, who followed him there in 1805, says "the population of this island, when compared with its size, is very small." (Voyage, p. 193.) After the "minutest research" at that time he found that it amounted only to four thousand souls. It is much less now; probably not more than fifteen hundred.

Of course it is easy to know the number of those within the immediate jurisdiction of the company. This is determined by a census from time to time. Even here the aborigines are the most numerous. Then come the Creoles, and last the Russians. But here you must bear in mind a distinction with regard to the former persons. In Spanish America all born there of European parentage are "Creoles;" in Russian America this term is applicable only to those whose parents are European and native, in other words "half-breeds." According to Wrangel, in 1839, the census of dependents of the company in all its districts was 246 Russians, 684 Creoles, and 8,882 Aleutians and Kodiaks, being in all 9,812. Of these 4,918 were men and 4,804 were women. Here the number of Russians is small. There is another report a little later preserved by Wappäus, which is not materially different. In 1851, according to the report of the company, there was an increase of Russians and Creoles, with a corresponding diminution of aborigines; being 503 Russians, 1,703 Creoles, and 7,055 aborigines, in all 9,283. In 1857 there were 644 Russians, 1,903 Creoles, and 7,245 aborigines, in all 9,792, of whom 5,733 were men and 4,659 were women. The increase from 1851 to 1857 was only 500, or about one per cent. annually. In 1860 there were "some hundred" Russians, 2,000 Creoles, and 8,000 aborigines, amounting in all to 10,540, of whom 5,382 were men and 5,158 were women. I am thus particular with these details that you may see how stationary population has been even within the sphere of the company.

The number of Russians and Creoles in the whole colony at the present time cannot be more than 2,500. The number of aborigines under the direct government of the company may be 8,000. There remain also the mass of aborigines outside the jurisdiction of the company, and having only a temporary or casual contact with it for purposes of trade. In this respect they are not unlike the aborigines of the United States while in their tribal condition, described so often as "Indians not taxed." For the number of these outside aborigines I prefer to follow the authority of the recent work already quoted, *Les Peuples de la Russie*, according to which they are estimated at between forty and fifty thousand.

Secondly. In speaking of *character* I turn to a different class of materials. The early Russians here were not Pilgrims. They were mostly runaways, fleeing from justice. Langsdorf says that "the greater part of the inferior officers of the different settlements were Siberian criminals, malefactors, and adventurers of various kinds." (Voyages, vol. 2, p. 67.) Their single and exclusive business was the collection of furs, from which they obtained the name of Promüschleniks, or fur collectors. But the name very early acquired a bad odor. Here again we have the same Russian authority, who, after saying that the inhabitants of the distant islands are under the superintendence of a Promüschlenik, adds, "which is, in other words, under that of a rascal, by whom they are oppressed, tormented, and plundered in every possible way." (*Ibid.*, p. 70.) It must not be forgotten that this authentic portrait is not of our day.

The aborigines are all in common language called Esquimaux; but they differ essentially from the Esquimaux of Greenland, and they also differ among themselves. Though popularly known by this family name, they have as many divisions and subdivisions, with as many languages and idioms, as France once had. There are large groups, each with its own nationality and language, and there are smaller groups, each with its tribal idiom. In short, the great problem of language is repeated here. Its forms seem to be infinite. Scientific inquiry traces many to a single root, but practically they are different. Here is that confusion of tongues which yields only to the presence of civilization, and it becomes more remarkable, as the idiom is often confined to so small a circle.

If we look at them ethnographically we shall find two principal groups or races, the first scientifically known as Esquimaux, and the second as Indians. By another nomenclature, which has the sanction of authority and of usage, they are divided into Esquimaux, Aleutians, Kenaians, and Koloschians, being four distinct groups. The Esquimaux and Aleutians are said to be Mongolian in origin. According to a doubtful theory they passed from Asia to America by the succession of islands beginning on the coast of Japan and extending to Alaska, which for this purpose became a bridge between the two continents. The Kenaians and Koloschians are Indians, belonging to known American races; so that these four groups are ethnographically resolved into two, and the two are resolved popularly into one.

There are general influences more or less applicable to all these races. The climate is peculiar, and the natural features of the country are commanding. Cool summers and mild winters are favorable to the huntsman and fisherman. Lofty mountains, volcanic forms, large rivers, numerous islands, and an extensive sea-coast constitute the great book of nature for all to read. None are dull. Generally they are quick, intelligent, and ingenious, excelling in the chase and in navigation, managing a boat as the rider his horse, until the man and the boat seem to be one. Some are very skillful with tools and exhibit remarkable taste. The sea is bountiful and the land has its supplies. From these they are satisfied. Better still, there is something in their nature which does not altogether reject the improvements of civilization. Unlike our Indians, they are willing to learn. By a strange superstition, which still continues, these races derive their descent from different animals. Some are gentle and pacific; others are warlike. All, I fear, are slaveholders; some are cruel task-masters, others in the interior are reputed to be cannibals. But the country back from the sea-coast is still an undiscovered secret.

(1.) Looking at them in their ethnographical groups I begin with the *Esquimaux*, who popularly give their name to the whole. They number about seventeen thousand, and stretch along the indented coast from its eastern limit on the Frozen ocean to the mouth of the Copper river in 60° north latitude, excluding the peninsula of Alaska, occupied by the Aleutians, and the peninsula of Kenay, occupied by the Kenaians. More powerful races of Indian origin, following the courses of the great rivers northward and westward, have gradually crowded the Esquimaux from the interior, until they constitute a belt on the salt water, including the islands of the coast, and especially Kodiak. Their various dialects are traced to a common root, while the prevailing language betrays an affinity with the Esquimaux of Greenland, and the intervening country watered by the Mackenzie. They share the characteristics of that extensive family, which, besides spreading across the continent, occupies an extent of sea-coast greater than any other people of the globe, from which their simple navigation has sallied forth so as to give them the name of Phœnicians of the North. Words exclusively belonging to the Esquimaux are found in the dialects of other races completely strangers to them, as Phœnician sounds are observed in the Celtic speech of Ireland.

The most known of the Russian Esquimaux is the small tribe now remaining on the island of Kodiak, which from the beginning has been a center of trade. Although by various intermixture they already approach the Indians of the coast, losing the Asiatic type, their speech remains as a distinctive sign of their race. They are Esquimaux, and I describe them in order to give an idea of this people.

The men are tall, with copper skins, small black eyes, flat faces, and teeth of dazzling whiteness. Once the women pierced the nostrils, the lower lip, and the ears for ornaments; but now only the nostrils are pierced. The aboriginal costume is still preserved, especially out of doors. Their food is mostly from the sea, without the roots or berries which the island supplies. The flesh and oil of the whale are a special luxury. The oil is drunk pure or to season other food. Accustomed to prolonged abstinence, they exhibit at times an appetite amounting to prodigy. In one night six men were able to devour the whole of a large bear. A strong drink made from the strawberry and myrtle, producing the effect of opium, has yielded to brandy. Sugar and tea are highly esteemed; but snuff is a delight. Lisiansky, records that they would go out of their way twenty miles merely for a pinch of snuff. They have tools of their own, which they use with skill. Their baidars, or canoes, are distinguished for completeness of finish and beauty of form. Unlike those of the Koloschians, lower down on the coast, which are hollowed from the trunks of trees, they are of seal skins stretched on frames, with a single aperture in the covering to receive the person of the master. The same skill appears in the carving of wood, whalebone. and walrus ivory. Their general mode of life is said. to be like that of other tribes on the coast. To all else they add a knowledge of the healing art and a passion for gaming.

Opposite to Kodiak, on the main land to the east, are the Tshugatchi, a kindred tribe, speaking the same language, but a different dialect. To the north is a succession of kindred tribes, differing in speech, and each with local peculiarities, but all are represented as kind, courteous, hospitable, and merry. It is a good sign that merriment should prevail. Their tribal names are derived from a neighboring river or some climatic circumstance. Thus, for instance, those on the mighty Kwichpak have the name of Kwichpakmutes, or "inhabitants of the great river." Those on Bristol bay are called by their cousins of Norton sound Akhkongbmutes, or "inhabitants of the warm country;" and the same designation is applied to the Kodiaks. Warmth, like other things in this world, is comparative, and to an Esquimaux at 64° north latitude another five degrees further south is in a "warm country." These northern tribes have been visited lately by our Telegraphic Exploring Expedition, who report especially their geographical knowledge and good disposition. As the remains of Major Kennicott descended the Kwichpak they were not without sympathy from the natives. Curiosity also had its part. At a village where the boat rested for the night the chief announced that it was the first time white men had ever been seen there.

(2.) The *Aleutians*, sometimes called Western Esquimaux, number about three thousand. By a plain exaggeration Knight, in his *Cyclopedia of Geography*, puts them at twenty thousand. Their home is the archipelago of volcanic islands, whose name they bear, and also a portion of the contiguous peninsula of Alaska.

The well-defined type has already disappeared; but the national dress continues still. This is a long shirt with tight sleeves, made from the skins of birds, either the sea-parrot or the diver. This dress, which is called the parka, is indispensable as clothing, blanket, and even as habitation during a voyage, being a complete shelter against wind and cold. They, too, are fishermen and huntsmen; but they seem to excel as artificers. Their instruments and utensils have been noted for beauty, and their baidars were pronounced by Sauer "infinitely superior to those of any other island." Still another navigator declares them to be "the best means yet discovered to go from place to place, either upon the deepest or shallowest water, in the quickest, easiest, and safest manner possible." (Langsdorf's Voyage, vol. 1, p. 48.) These illustrate their nature, which is finer than that of their neighbors. They are at home on the water, and excite admiration by the skill with which they manage their elegant craft, so that Admiral Lütke recognized them as Cossacks of the sea. Ounalaska is the principal of these islands, and from the time they were first visited seems to have excited a peculiar interest. Captain Cook painted it kindly; so have succeeding navigators. And here have lived the islanders who seem to have given to navigators a new experience. Alluding especially to them, the reporter of Billings's voyage says: "The capacity of the natives of these islands infinitely surpasses every idea that I had formed of the abilities of savages." (P. 273.) There is another remark of this authority which shows how they had yielded, even in their favorite dress, to the demands of commerce. After saying that formerly they had worn garments of sea otter, he pathetically adds, "but not since the Russians have had any intercourse with them." (P. 155.) Poor islanders! Exchanging choice furs, once their daily wear, for meaner skins.

(3.) The *Kenaians*, numbering as many as twenty-five thousand, take their common name from the peninsula of Kenay, with Cook's inlet on the north and Prince William sound on the south. Numerous beyond any other family in Russian America, they belong to a widespread and teeming Indian race, which occupies all the northern interior of the continent, stretching from Hudson bay in the east to the Esquimaux in the west. This is the great nation called sometimes Athabascan, or from the native name of the Rocky mountains, on whose flanks they live, Chepewyan, but more properly designated as Tinneh, with branches in southern Oregon and northern California, and then again with other offshoots, known as the Apaches and Navajoes, in Arizona, New Mexico, and Chihuahua, more than thirty parallels of latitude from the parent stem. Of this extended race, the northwestern branch, known to travelers as Loucheux, and in their own tongue as Kutchin, after occupying the inner portion of Russian America on the Youkon and the Porcupine reached the sea-coast at Cook's inlet, where it appears under the name of Kenaians. The latter are said to bear about the same relation in language and intellectual development to the entire group as the islanders of Kodiak bear to the Esquimaux.

The Kenaians call themselves in their own dialect by yet another name, Thnainas, meaning men; thus by a somewhat boastful designation asserting manhood. Their features and complexion associate them with the red men of America, as does their speech. The first to visit them was Cook, and he was struck by the largeness of their heads, which seemed to him disproportioned to the rest of the body. They were strong-chested also, with thick short necks, sprending faces, eyes inclined to be small, white teeth, black hair, and thin beard. Their persons seemed to be clean and decent, without grease or dirt. In dress they were thought to resemble the people of Greenland. Their boats had a similar affinity. But in these particulars they were not unlike the other races _ have already described. They were clothed in the skins of animals with the fur outward, or sometimes in the skins of birds, over which, as a protection against rain, was worn a frock made from the intestines of the whale and resembling the gold-beater leaf, as was observed by Behring in his early voyage. Their boats were of seal skin stretched on frames, and were of different sizes. In one of these Cook counted twenty women and one man, besides children. At that time, though thievish in propensity, they were not unamiable. Shortly afterwards they were reported by Russian traders, who had much to do with them, as "good people," who behaved "in a very friendly manner." (Billing's Voyage, p. 197.) I do not know that they have lost this character since.

Here, too, is the accustomed multiplicity of tribes, each with its idiom, and sometimes differing in religious superstition, especially on the grave question of descent from the dog or the crow. There is also a prevailing usage for the men of one tribe to choose their wives from another tribe, when the tribal character of the mother attaches to the offspring, which is another illustration of the law of slavery *partus sequitur ventrem*. The late departure from this usage is quoted by the old men as a sufficient reason for the mortality which has afflicted the Kenaians, although a better reason may be found in the ravages of the small-pox, unhappily introduced by the Russians. In 1838 ten thousand persons on the coast are reported to have fallen victims to this disease.

(4.) Last of the four races are the *Koloschians*, numbering about four thousand, who occupy the coast and islands from the mouth of the Copper river to the southern boundary of Russian America, making about sixteen settlements. They belong to an Indian group extending as far south as the Straits of Fuca, and estimated to contain twenty-five thousand souls. La Pérouse, after considerable experience of the aborigines on the Atlantic coast, asserts that those whom he saw here are not Esquimaux. (Voyage, Tom. 2, p. 205.) The name seems to be of Russian origin, and is equivalent to Indian. Here again is another variety of languages and as many separate nations. Near Mount St. Elias are the Jacoutats, who are the least known; then came the Thlinkitts, who occupy the islands and coast near Sitka, and are known in Oregon under the name of Stikines; and then again we have the Kaigans, who, beginning on Russian territory, overlap Queen Charlotte's island, beneath the British flag. All these, with their subdivisions, are Koloschians; but every tribe or nation has four different divisions, derived from four different animals, the whale, the eagle, the crow, and the wolf, which are so many heraldic devices, marking distinct groups.

There are points already noticed in the more northern groups which are repeated here. As among the Kenaians husband and wife are of different animal devices. A crow cannot marry a crow. There is the same skill in the construction of canoes; but the stretched seal skin gives place here to the trunk of a tree shaped and hollowed so that it will sometimes hold forty persons. There are good qualities among the Aleutians which the Koloschians do not possess, but they have, perhaps, a stronger sense. They are of constant courage. As daring navigators they are unsurpassed, sailing six or seven hundred miles in their open canoes. Some are thrifty, and show a sense of property. Some have developed an aptitude for trade unknown to their northern neighbors or to the Indians of the United States, and will work for wages, whether in tilling the ground or other employment. Their superior nature discards corporal punishment, even for boys, as an ignominy not to be endured. They believe in a Creator and in the immortality of the soul. But here a mystic fable is woven into their faith. The spirits of heroes dead in battle are placed in the sky and appear in the Aurora Borealis. Long ago a deluge occurred, when the human family was saved in a floating vessel, which, after the subsidence of the waters, struck on a rock and broke in halves. The Koloschians represent one half of the vessel, and the rest of the world the other half. Such is that pride of race which civilization does not always efface.

For generations they have been warriors, prompt to take offense and vindictive, as is the nature of the Indian race—always ready to exact an eye for an eye and a tooth for a tooth. This character has not changed. As was the case once in Italy, the dagger is an inseparable companion. Private quarrels are common. The duel is an institution. So is slavery still, having a triple origin in war, purchase, or birth. The slave is only a dog, and must obey his master in all things, even to taking the life of another. He is without civil rights; he cannot marry or possess anything; he can eat only the offal of another, and his body, when released by death, is thrown into the sea. A chief sometimes sacrifices his slaves, and then another chief seeks to outdo him in this inhumanity. All this is indignantly described by Sir Edward Belcher and Sir George Simpson. But a slave once a freedman has all the rights of a Koloschian. Here, too, are the distinctions of wealth. The rich paint their faces daily; the poor renew the paint only when the colors begin to disappear.

These are the same people who for more than a century have been a terror on this coast. It was Koloschians who received the two boats' crews of the Russian discoverer in 1741, as they landed in one of its wooded coves, and no survivor returned to tell their fate. They were the actors in another tragedy at the beginning of the century, when the Russian fort at Sitka was stormed and its defenders put to death, some with excruciating torture. Lisiansky, whose visit was shortly afterward, found them "a shrewd, bold, though perfidious people," whose chiefs used "very sublime expressions," and swore oaths, like that of Demosthenes, by their ancestors living and dead, "calling heaven, earth, sun, moon, and stars to witness, particularly when they want to deceive." (Voyage, p. 16.) Since then the fort has been repeatedly threatened by these warriors, who multiply by reinforcements from the interior, so that the governor in 1837 said, "Although seven hundred only are now in the neighborhood seven thousand may arrive in a few hours." (Belcher's Voyage, vol. 1, p. 94.) A little later their constant character was recognized by Sir George Simpson, when he pronounced them "numerous, treacherous, and fierce," in contrast with Aleutians, whom he describes as "peaceful even to cowardice." And yet this fighting race is not entirely indocile, if we may credit recent report, that its warriors are changing to traders.

Climate.

III. From population I pass to *Climate*, which is more important, as it is a constant force. Climate is the key to this whole region. It is the governing power which rules production and life, for nature and man each must conform to its laws. Here at last the observations of science give to our inquiry a solid support.

Montesquieu has a famous chapter on the influence of climate over the customs and institutions of a people. Conclusions which in his day were regarded as visionary or far-fetched are now unquestioned truth. Climate is a universal master. But nowhere, perhaps, does it appear more eccentric than in the southern portion of Russian America. Without a knowledge of climatic laws the weather here would seem like a freak of nature. But a brief explanation shows how all its peculiarities are the result of natural causes, which operate with a force as unerring as gravitation. Heat

and cold, rain and fog, to say nothing of snow and ice, which play such a part in this region, are not abnormal, but according to law.

This law has been known only of late years. Even so ingenious an inquirer as Captain Cook notices the mildness of the climate without attempting to account for it. He records that in his opinion "cattle might exist in Ounalaska all the year round without being housed," (Voyages, vol. 2, p. 520;) and this was in latitude 53° 52′, on the same parallel with Labrador, and several degrees north of Quebec; but he stops with a simple statement of the suggestive fact. This, however, was inconsistent with the received idea at the time. A geographer, who wrote just before Cook sailed, has a chapter to show that the climate of Quebec continues across the continent, and by a natural consequence that America is colder than Asia. I refer to the *Mémoires Géographiques* of Engel, (page 196.) He would have been astonished had he seen the revelations of an isothermal map, showing that precisely the reverse is true; that the climate of Quebec does not continue across the continent; that the Pacific coast of our continent is warmer than the corresponding Atlantic coast, and that America is warmer than Asia, so far at least as can be determined by the two opposite coasts. Such is the unquestionable truth, of which there are plentiful signs. The Flora on the American side, even in Behring straits, is more vigorous than that on the Asiatic side; the American mountains have less snow than their Asiatic neighbors. Among many illustrations of the temperature I know none more direct than that furnished by the late Hon. William Sturgis, of Boston, who was familiar with the northwest coast at the beginning of the century, in a lecture on the Oregon question in 1845. After remarking that the climate there is "altogether milder and the winter less severe than in corresponding latitudes on this side of the continent," he proceeds to testify that, "as a proof of its mildness, he had passed seven winters between the latitudes of 51° and 57°, frequently lying so near the shore as to have a small cable fast to the trees, and only once was his ship surrounded by ice sufficiently firm to bear the weight of a man." But this intelligent navigator assigns no reason. To the common observer it seemed as if the temperature grew milder traveling with the sun until it dipped in the ocean.

Among the authorities open before me I quote two, which show that this difference of temperature between the Atlantic and Pacific coasts was imagined, if not actually recognized, during the last century. Portlock, the Englishman, who was on this coast in 1787, after saying that during stormy and unsettled weather the air had been mild and temperate, remarks that he is "inclined to think that the climate here is not so severe as has been generally supposed." (Voyage, p. 188.) La Pérouse, the Frenchman, who was here the same year, and had been before in Hudson bay, on the other side of the continent, says still more explicitly that "the climate of this coast appeared to' him infinitely milder than that of Hudson bay in the same latitude, and that the pines which he had measured here were much larger." (Voyage. vol. 2, p. 187.) Langsdorf, when at Sitka in 1806, records that Mr. John D. Wolf. a citizen of the United States, who had passed the winter at the settlement, "is much surprised at finding the cold less severe than at Boston, Rhode Island, and other Provinces of the United States which lie more to the South." (Voyages, vol. 2, p. 101.) .

All this is now explained by certain known forces in nature. Of these the most important is a thermal current in the Pacific, corresponding to the Gulf Stream in the Atlantic. The latter, having its origin in the heated waters of the Gulf of Mexico, flows as a river through the ocean northward, encircling England, bathing Norway, and warming all within its influence. A similar stream in the Pacific, sometimes called the Japanese current. having its origin under the equator near the Philippines and the Malaccas, amid no common heats, after washing the ancient empire of Japan sweeps northward until, forming two branches, one moves onward to Behring straits and the other bends eastward along the Aleutian islands, and then southward along the coast of Sitka, Oregon, and California. Geographers have described this "heater," which in the lower latitudes is as high as 81° of Fahrenheit, and even far to the north it is as high as 50°. A chart now before me in Findlay's *Pacific Ocean Directory* portrays its course as it warms so many islands and such an extent of coast. An officer of the United States Navy, Lieutenant Bent, in a paper before the Geographical Society of New York, while exhibiting the influence of this current in mitigating the climate of the northwest coast, mentions that vessels on the Asiatic side, becoming unwieldy with accumulations of ice on the hull and rigging, run over to the higher latitude on the American side and "thaw out." But the tepid waters which melt the ice on a vessel must change the atmosphere wherever they flow.

I hope you will not regard the illustration as too familiar if I remind you that in the economy of a household pipes of hot water are sometimes employed in tempering the atmosphere by heat carried from below to rooms above. In the economy of nature these thermal currents are only pipes of hot water, modifying the climate of continents by carrying heat from the warm cisterns of the South into the most distant places of the north. So also there are sometimes pipes of hot air, having a similar purpose; and these, too, are found in this region. Every ocean wind, from every quarter, as it traverses the stream of heat, takes up the warmth and carries it to the coast, so that the oceanic current is reënforced by an aerial current of constant influence.

But these forces are aided essentially by the configuration of the northwest coast, with a lofty and impenetrable barricade of mountains, by which its islands and harbors are protected from the cold of the north. Occupying the Aleutian islands, traversing the peninsula of Alaska, and running along the margin of the ocean to the latitude of 54° 40', this mountain ridge is a climatic division, or, according to a German geographer, a "climatic shed," such as perhaps exists nowhere else in the world. Here are Alps, some of them volcanic, with Mount St. Elias higher than Mont Blanc, standing on guard against the Arctic Circle. So it seems even without the aid of science. Here is a dike between the icy waters of Behring sea and the milder Southern ocean. Here is a partition between the treeless northern coast and the wooded coast of the Kenaians and Koloschians. Here is a fence which separates the animal kingdom of this region, leaving on one side the walrus and ice-fox from the Frozen ocean and on the other side the humming bird from the tropics. I simply repeat the statements of geography. And now you will not fail to observe how by this configuration the thermal currents of ocean and air are left to exercise all their climatic power.

There is one other climatic incident here, which is now easily explained. Early navigators record the prevailing moisture. All are enveloped in fog. Behring names an island Foggy. Another gives the same designation to a cape at the southern extremity of Russian America. Cook records fog. La Pérouse speaks of continued rain and fog in the month of August. And now visitors, whether for science or business, make the same report. The forests testify also. According to Physical Geography it could not be otherwise. The warm air from the ocean encountering the snow-capped mountains would naturally produce this result. Rain is nothing but atmosphere condensed and falling in drops to the earth. Fog is atmosphere still held in solution, but so far condensed as to become visible. This condensation occurs when the air is chilled by contact with a colder atmosphere. Now, these very conditions occur on the northwest coast. The ocean air, as it comes in contact with the elevated range, is chilled until its moisture is set free.

Add to these influences, especially as regards Sitka, the presence of mountain masses and of dense forests, all tending to make this coast warmer in winter and colder in summer than it would otherwise be.

Practical observation has verified these conclusions of science. Any isothermal map is enough for our purpose; but there are others which show the relative conditions generally of different portions of the globe. I ask attention to those of Keith Johnston, in his admirable atlas. But I am glad to present a climatic table of the Pacific coast in comparison with the Atlantic coast, which has been recently compiled, at my request, from the archives of the Smithsonian Institution with permission of its learned secretary, by a collaborator of the Institution, who visited Russian America under the auspices of the Telegraph Company. In studying this table we shall be able to comprehend the relative position of this region in the physical geography of the world:

	Mean Temperature in Degrees Fahrenheit.					Precipitation in Rain or Snow. Depth in Inches.				
	Spring.	Summer.	Autumn.	Winter.	Year.	Spring.	Summer.	Autumn.	Winter.	Year.
St. Michaels, Russian America. Lat. 63° 28' 45" North.	28.75	52.25	27.00	7.00	27.48	-	-	-	-	-
Fort Youkon, Russian America. Lat. (near) 67°.	14.22	59.67	17.37	23.80	16.92	-	-	-	-	-
Ikogmut, Russian America. Lat. 61° 47'.	19.62	49.32	36.05	0.95	24.57	-	-	-	-	-
Sitka, Russian America. Lat. 57° 03'.	39.65	53.37	43.80	32.30	42.12	18.32	15.75	32.10	23.77	89.94
Puget sound, Washington Territory. Lat. 47° 07'.	48.88	63.44	51.30	39.38	50.75	7.52	3.68	15.13	20.65	46.98
Astoria, Oregon. Lat. 46° 11'.	51.16	61.36	53.55	42.43	52.13	16.43	4.85	21.77	44.15	87.20
San Francisco, California. Lat. 37° 48'.	55.39	58.98	58.29	50.25	55.73	6.65	0.09	2.69	13.40	22.92
Nain, Labrador. Lat. 57° 10'.	23.67	48.57	33.65	0.40	26.40	-	-	-	-	-
Montreal, Canada East. Lat. 45° 30'.	41.20	68.53	44.93	16.40	42.77	7.66	11.20	7.42	.72	27.00
Portland, Maine. Lat. 43° 39'.	40.12	63.75	45.75	21.52	42.78	-	-	-	-	-
Fort Hamilton, New York. Lat. 40° 37'.	47.84	71.35	55.79	32.32	51.82	11.69	11.64	9.88	10.31	43.22
Washington, District of Columbia.	54.19	73.07	53.91	33.57	53.69	10.48	10.53	10.16	10.06	41.24

It will be seen from this table that the winters of Sitka are relatively warm, not differing much from those of Washington, and several degrees warmer than those of New York; but the summers are colder. The mean temperature of winter is 32° 30', while that of summer is 53° 37'. The Washington winter is 38° 57'; the Washington summer is 73° 07'. These points exhibit the peculiarities of this coast—warm winters and cool summers.

The winter of Sitka is milder than that of many European capitals. It is much milder than that of St. Petersburg, Moscow, Stockholm, Copenhagen, Berne, or Berlin. It is milder even than that of Manheim, Stuttgard, Vienna, Sebastopol in the Crimea, or Turin. It is not much colder than that of Padua. According to observations at Sitka in 1831 it froze for only two days in December and seven days in January. In February the longest frost lasted five days: in March it did not freeze during the day at all, and rarely in the night. During the next winter the thermometer did not fall below 21° Fahrenheit; in January, 1834, it reached 11°. On the other hand a temperature of 50° has been noted in January. The roadstead is open throughout the year, and only a few land-locked bays are frozen.

The prevailing dampness at Sitka makes a residence there far from agreeable, although it does not appear to be injurious to health. England is also damp, but Englishmen boast that theirs is the best climate of the world. At Sitka the annual fall of rain is eighty-nine inches. The mean annual fall in all England is forty inches, although in mountainous districts of Cumberland and Westmoreland the fall amounts to ninety and even one hundred and forty inches. In Washington it is forty-one inches. The forests at Sitka are so wet that they will not burn, although frequent attempts have been made to set them on fire. The houses, which are of wood, suffer from the constant moisture. In 1828, there were twenty days when it rained or snowed continuously; one hundred and twenty when it rained or snowed part of the day, and only sixty-six days of clear weather. Some years only forty bright days have been counted. Hinds, the naturalist, records only thirty-seven "really clear and fine days." A scientific observer who was there last year counted sixty. A visitor for fourteen days found only two when nautical observations could be made; but these were as fine as he had ever known in any country.

The whole coast from Sitka to the peninsula of Alaska seems to have the same continuous climate, whether as regards temperature or moisture. The island of Kodiak and the recess of Cook's inlet are outside of this climatic curve, so as to be comparatively dry. Langsdorf reports the winters "frequently so mild in the lower parts of Kodiak that the snow does not lie upon the ground for any length of time, nor is anything like severe cold felt." The Aleutian islands, further west, are somewhat colder than Sitka, although the difference is not great. The summer temperature is seldom above 66°; the winter temperature is more seldom as low as 2° below zero. The snow falls about the beginning of October, and is seen sometimes as late as the end of April; but it does not remain long on the surface. The mean temperature of Ounalaska is about 40°. Chamisso found the temperature of spring water at the beginning of the year to be 38° 50'. There are some years when it rains on this island the whole winter. The fogs prevail from April till the middle of July, when they seem for the time to be driven further north. The islands northward toward Behring straits are proportionately colder, but you will not forget that the American coast is milder than the opposite coast of Asia.

From Mr. Bannister I have an authentic statement with regard to the temperature north of the Aleutians, as observed by himself in the autumn of 1865 and the months following. Even here the winter does not seem so terrible as is sometimes imagined. During most of the time work could be done with comfort in the open air. It was only when it stormed that the men were kept within doors. In transporting supplies from St. Michaels to Nulato, a distance of two hundred and fifty miles, they found no hardship, even when obliged to bivouac in the open air.

On Norton sound and the Kwichpak river winter may be said to commence at the end of September, although the weather is not severe till the end of October. The first snow falls about the 20th or 25th September. All the small ponds and lakes were frozen early in October. The Kwichpak was frozen solid about the 20th or 25th of this month. On the 1st November the harbor at St. Michaels was still open, but on the morning of the 4th it was frozen solid enough for sledges to cross on the ice. In December there were two thaws, one of them accompanied by rain for a day. The snow was about two feet deep at the end of the month. January was uniformly cold, and it was said that at one place sixty-five miles northeast of St. Michaels the thermometer descended to 58° below zero. February was unusually mild all over the country. In the middle of the month there was an extensive thaw, with showers of

rain. About half of the snow disappeared, leaving much of the ground bare. March was pleasant, without very cold weather. Its mean temperature was 20°,; its minimum was 3° below zero.

Spring commences on the Kwichpak the 1st May, or a few days later, when the birds return and vegetation begins to appear. The ice did not entirely disappear from the river till after the 20th May. The sea ice continued in the bay of St. Michaels as late as 1st June. The summer temperature is much higher in the interior of the country than on the coast. Parties traveling on the Kwichpak in June complained sometimes from the heat.

The river Youkon, which, flowing into the Kwichpak, helps to swell that stream, is navigable for at least four, if not five, months in the year. The thermometer at Fort Youkon is sometimes at 65° below zero of Fahrenheit. and for three months of a recent winter it stood at 50° below zero without variation. In summer it rises above 80° in the shade; but a hard frost occurs at times in August. The southwest wind brings warmth; the northeast wind brings cold. Some years there is, no rain for months, and then again showers alternate with sunshine. The snow packs hard at an average of two and a half feet deep. The ice is four or five feet thick; in a severe winter it is six feet thick. Life at Fort Youkon under these rigors of nature, although not inviting, is not intolerable.

Such is the climate of this extensive region, so far as is known, along its coast, among its islands, and on its great rivers, from its southern limits to its most northern ice, with contrasts and varieties such as Milton describes:

"For hot, cold, moist and dry, four champions fierce
Strive here for mastery."

Vegetable Products.

IV. *Vegetable Products* depend upon climate. They are determined by its laws. Therefore what has been already said upon the one prepares the way for the consideration of the other: and here we have the reports of navigators and the suggestions of science.

From the time this coast was first visited navigators reported the aspects which nature assumed. But their opportunities were casual, and they were obliged to confine themselves to what was most obvious. As civilization did not exist, the only vegetable products were indigenous to the soil. These were trees, berries, and plants. At the first landing, on the discovery of the coast by Behring, Steller found among the provisions in one of the Indian cabins "a sweet herb" dressed for food in the same manner as in Kamtschatka." That "sweet herb" is the first vegetable production of which we have any record on this coast. At the same time, although ashore only six hours, this naturalist "gathered herbs and brought such a quantity to the ship that the describing of them took him a considerable time." This description it is said was adopted afterwards in the *Flora Siberica*.

Trees were noticed even before landing. They enter into descriptions, and are often introduced to increase the savage wildness of the scene. La Pérouse doubts "if the deep valleys of the Alps and the Pyrenees present a picture so frightful and at the same time so picturesque, which would deserve to be visited by the curious if it were not at one of the extremities of the earth." (Tom. 2, page 191.) Lisiansky, as he approached the coast of Sitka, records that "nothing presented itself to the view but impenetrable woods reaching from the water side to the very tops of the highest mountains, so wild and gloomy that they appeared more adapted for the residence of wild beasts than of men." (Page 145.) Lütke portrays the "savage and picturesque aspect" of the whole northwest coast. (Tom. 1, page 101.)

As navigators landed they saw nature in detail; and here they were impressed by the size of the trees. Cook finds at Prince William sound "Canada and spruce pine, some of them tolerably large." La Pérouse alludes to trees more than once. He describes pines measuring six feet in diameter and one hundred and forty feet in height, and then again introduces us to "those superb pines fit for the masts of our largest vessels." Portlock notices in Cook's inlet "wood of different kinds in great abundance, such as pine, black birch, witch hazel, and poplar; many of the pines large enough for lower masts to a ship of four hundred tons burden;" and then again at Port Etches he noticed "trees of the pine kind, some very large, a good quantity of alder, a kind of hazel, but not larger than will do for making handspikes." Meares reports "woods thick," also "the black pine in great plenty, capable of making excellent spars." Vancouver reports in latitude 60° 1′ "a woodland country." Sauer, who was there a little later, in the expedition of Billings, saw trees six feet in diameter and one hundred and fifty feet in height, "excellent wood for ship-building." In Prince William sound the ship "took in a variety of fine spars," and he proceeds to say, "The timber comprised a variety of pines of immense thickness and height, some entirely tough and fibrous, and of these we made our best oars." Lisiansky says that at Kodiak "for want of fir he made a new bowsprit of one of the pine trees, which answered admirably." Lütke testifies to the "magnificent pine and fir" at Sitka, adding what seems an inconsistent judgment with regard to its durability. Belcher notices Garden island, in latitude 60° 21′, as "covered with pine trees;" and then again at Sitka speaks of a "very fine-grained bright yellow cypress as the most valuable wood, which, besides being used in boats, was exported to the Sandwich islands in return especially for Chinese goods."

Turning westward from Cook's inlet the forests on the sea line are rarer until they entirely disappear. The first settlement on the island of Kodiak was on the southwestern coast, but the want of timber there caused its transfer to the northeastern coast, where there are "considerable forests of fine tall trees." But where trees are wanting grass seems to abound. This is the case with Kodiak, the peninsula of Alaska, and the Aleutian islands generally. Of these Ounalaska, libeled by the immortal verse of Campbell, has been the most described. This well-known island is without trees; but it seems singularly adapted to the growth of grass, which is often so high as to impede the traveler and to over-top even the willows. The mountains themselves are for a considerable distance clothed with rich turf. One of these scenes is represented in a print which you will find among the views of the vegetation of the Pacific in the London reproduction of the work of Kittlitz. This peculiarity was first noticed by Cook, who says, with a sailor sententiousness, that he did not see there "a single stick of wood of any size," but "plenty of grass very thick and to a great length." Lütke records that after leaving Brazil he met nothing so agreeable as the grass of this island.

North of Alaska, on Behring sea, the forests do not approach the coast, except at the heads of bays and sounds, although they abound in the interior, and extend even to within a short distance of the Frozen ocean. Such is the personal testimony of a scientific observer who has recently returned from this region. In Norton's sound Cook, who was the first to visit it, reports "a coast covered with wood, an agreeable sight," and, on walking in the country, "small spruce trees, none more than six or eight inches in diameter." The next day he sent men ashore "to cut brooms, which he needed, and the branches of spruce trees for brewing beer." On the Kwichpak and its affluent, the Youkon, trees are sometimes as high as a hundred feet. The supply of timber at St. Michaels is from the drift wood of the river. Near Fort Youkon, at the junction of the Porcupine and the Youkon, are forests of pine, poplar, willow, and birch. The pine is the most plentiful; but the small islands in the great river are covered with poplar and willow. Immense trunks rolling under the fort show that there must be large trees nearer the headwaters.

But even in northern latitudes the American coast is not without vegetation. Grass here takes the place of trees. At Fort Youkon, in latitude 67°, there is "a thin, wiry grass." Navigators notice the contrast between the opposite coasts of the two continents. Kotzebue, while in Behring straits, where the two approach each other, was struck by black, mossy rocks frowning with snow and icicles on the Asiatic side, while on the American side "even the summits of the highest mountains were free from snow, and the coast was covered with a green carpet." (Voyage, vol. 1, p. 249.) But the contrast with the Atlantic coast

of the continent is hardly less. The northern
limit of trees is full seven degrees higher in
Russian America than in Labrador. In point
of fact, on the Atlantic coast, in latitude 57°
58′, which is that of Sitka, there are no trees.
All this is most suggestive.

Next after trees early navigators speak often-
est of *berries*, which they found in profusion. Not a sailor lands who does not find
them. Cook reports "berries" on Norton
sound, and "a great variety" at Ounalaska.
Portlock finds at Port Etches "fruit bushes in
great abundance, such as bilberry, raspberry,
strawberry, and currant, red and black." At
Prince William sound "any quantity might be
gathered for a winter stock." Meares saw
there "a few black currant bushes." Billings
finds at Kodiak "several species of berries,
with currants and raspberries in abundance, the
latter white, but extremely large, being bigger
than a mulberry." Langsdorf finds all these
at Ounalaska, with whortleberries and cran-
berries besides. Belcher reports at Garden
island "strawberries, pigeon berries, whortleberries, and a small cranberry in tolerable
profusion, without going in search of them."
All these I quote precisely, and in the order
of time.

Next to berries were *plants* for food; and
these were in constant abundance. Behring,
on landing at the Shumagin islands, observed
the natives "to eat roots which they dug out
of the ground, and scarce shaked off the earth
before they eat them." Cook reports at Ounalaska "a great variety of plants, such as are
found in Europe and other parts of America,
particularly Newfoundland, one of which was
like parsley and eat very well, either in soups
or salads." La Pérouse, who landed in latitude 58° 37, finds a French bill of fare, including celery, chicory, sorrel, and "almost
all that exists in the meadows and mountains
of France," besides several grains for forage.
Every day and each meal the ship's kettle was
filled with these supplies, and all eat them in
soups, ragouts, and salads, much to the benefit of their health. Portlock reports at Port
Etches, besides water-cresses, "just above the
beach, between the bay and the lake, a piece
of wild wheat, about two hundred yards long
and five yards broad, growing at least two feet
high, which with proper care might certainly be
made a useful article of food;" at Cook's inlet
he reports "ginseng and snakeroot." Meares
reports at Prince William sound "snakeroot
and ginseng, some of which the natives have
always with them as a medicine." Billings finds
at Kodiak "ginseng, wild onions, and the edi-
ble roots of Kamtschatka;" and then again in
Prince William sound he finds "plenty of ginseng and some snakeroot." Vancouver finds
at Cape Phipps "wild vegetables in great abundance." Langsdorf adds to the list at Ounalaska "Siberian parsnip, or sweet plant."
These, too, I quote precisely, and in the
order of time.

Since the establishment of Europeans on this

coast an attempt has been made to introduce
the nutritious grains and vegetables known to
the civilized world; but without very brilliant
success. Against wheat and rye and against
orchard fruits there are obstacles of climate,
perhaps insuperable. All these require summer heat: but here the summer is comparatively cold. The northern limit of wheat is
several degrees below the southern limit of
these possessions, so that this friendly grain
is out of the question. Rye flourishes further
north, as do oats also. The supposed northern
limit of these grains embraces Sitka and grazes
the Aleutian islands. But there are other
climatic conditions which are wanting at least
for rye. One of these is dry weather, which is
required at the time of its bloom. Possibly
the clearing of the forest may produce some
modification of the weather. For the present
barley grows better, and there is reason to believe that it may be cultivated successfully very
far to the north. It has ripened at Kodiak.
There are many garden vegetables which have
become domesticated. Lütke reports that at
Sitka potatoes flourish; so that all have enough.
Langsdorf reports the same of Kodiak. There
are also radishes, cabbages, cauliflowers, peas,
and carrots—making a very respectable list.
The same, perhaps, may be found at Ounalaska.
On Norton sound I hear of radishes, beets,
and cabbages. Even as far north as Fort
Youkon, on the parallel of 67°, potatoes, peas,
turnips, and even barley have been grown; but
the turnips were unfit for the table, being rot-
ten at the heart. A recent resident reports
that there are no fruit trees, and not even a
raspberry bush, and that he lost all his potatoes
during one season by a frost in the latter days
of July; but do not forget that these potatoes
were the wall-flowers of the Arctic Circle.

Thus it appears that the vegetable productions of the country are represented practically by trees. The forests which overshadow
the coast from Sitka to Cook's inlet are all that
we can show under this head out of which a
revenue can be derived, unless we add ginseng,
which is so much prized by the Chinese, and
perhaps also snakeroot. Other things may
contribute to the scanty support of a household; but timber will in all probability be an
article of commerce. It has been so already.
Ships from the Sandwich islands have come
for it, and there is reason to believe that this
trade may be extended indefinitely, so that
Russian America may be on the Pacific like
Maine on the Atlantic, and the lumbermen of
Sitka may vie with their hardy brethren of the
East.

Here a question occurs. These forests as
described seem to afford all that can be desired.
The trees are abundant, and they are perfect in
in size, not unlike

> "The tallest pine
> Hewn on Norwegian hills to be tho mast
> Of some great admiral."

But a doubt arises as to their commercial value.
Here we have the inconsistent testimony of

Lütke. According to him the pines and firs which he calls "magnificent" constitute an untried source of commercial wealth. Not only, California, but other countries poor in trees, like Mexico, the Sandwich islands, and even Chili will need them. And yet he does not conceal an unfavorable judgment of the timber, which as seen in the houses of Sitka, suffering from constant moisture, did not seem to be durable. (Voyage, Tom. 1, pp. 105, 151.) Sir Edward Belcher differs from the Russian admiral, for he praises especially the timber of "the higher latitudes, either for spars or plank." (Voyage, vol. 1, p. 300.) Perhaps its durability may depend upon the climate where it is used, so that the timber of this region may be lasting enough when transported to another climate. In the rarity of trees on the islands and mainland of the Pacific the natural supply is in Russian America. One of the early navigators even imagined that China must look this way, and he expected that "the woods would yield a handsome revenue when the Russian commerce with China should be established." American commerce with China is established. Perhaps timber may become one of its staples.

A profitable commerce in timber has already begun at Puget sound. By the official returns of 1866 it appears that it was exported to a long list of foreign countries and places, in which I find Victoria, Honolulu, Callao, Tahiti, Canton, Valparaiso, Adelaide, Hong Kong, Sydney, Montevideo, London, Melbourne, Shanghae, Peru, Coquimbo, Calcutta, Hilo, Cape Town, Cork, Guaymas, and Siam; and that in this commerce were employed no less than eighteen ships, thirty barks, four brigs, twenty-eight schooners, and ten steamers. The value of the lumber and spars exported abroad was over half a million dollars, while more than four times that amount was shipped coastwise. But the coasts of Russian America are darker with trees than those further south. The pines in which they abound do not flourish as low down as Puget sound. Northward, they are numerous and easily accessible.

In our day the Flora of the coast has been explored with care. Kittlitz, who saw it as a naturalist, portrays it with the enthusiasm of an early navigator; but he speaks with knowledge. He, too, dwells on the "surprising power and luxuriance" of the pine forests, describing them with critical skill. The trees which he identifies are the *Pinus Canadensis*, distinguished for its delicate foliage; the *Pinus Mertensiana*, a new species, rival of the other in height; and *Pinus Palustris*, growing in swampy declivities, and not attaining height. In the clearings or on the outskirts of thickets are shrubs, being chiefly a species of *Rubus*, with flowers of carmine and aromatic fruit. About and over all are mosses and lichens invigorated by the constant moisture, while colossal trees, undermined or uprooted, crowd the surface, reminding the scientific observer of the accumulations of the coal measures. Two different prints in the Loudon reproduction of the work of Kittlitz present pictures of these vegetable productions grouped for beauty and instruction. I refer to these and also to the Essay of Hinds on the *Regions of Vegetation*, the latter to be found at the end of the volumes containing Belcher's Voyage.

In turning from the vegetable products of this region, it will not be out of place if I refer for one moment to its domestic animals, for these are necessarily associated with such products. Some time ago it was stated that cattle had not flourished at Sitka owing to the want of proper pasturage and the difficulty of making hay in a climate of such moisture. Hogs are more easily sustained, but feeding on fish, instead of vegetable products, their flesh acquires a fishy taste, which does not recommend it. Nor has there been greater success with poultry, for this becomes the prey of the crow, whose voracity here is absolutely fabulous. A Koloschian tribe traces its origin to this bird, which in this neighborhood might be a fit progenitor. Not content with swooping upon hens and chickens it descends upon hogs to nibble at their tails, and so successfully "that the hogs here are without tails," and then it scours the streets so well that it is called the scavenger of Sitka. But there are other places more favored. The grass at Kodiak is well suited to cattle, and it is supposed that sheep would thrive there. The grass at Ounalaska is famous, and Cook thought the climate good for cattle, of which we have at least one illustration. Langsdorf reports that "a cow grazed there luxuriously for several years, and then was lost in the mountains." That grazing animal is a good witness. Perhaps also it is typical of the peaceful inhabitants.

Mineral Products.

V. In considering the *Mineral Products* I shall first ask attention to such indications as are afforded by the early navigators. They were not geologists. Indeed, geology was at that time unknown. They saw only what was exposed. And yet during the long interval that has elapsed not very much has been added to their conclusions. The existence of iron is hardly less uncertain now than then. The existence of copper is hardly more certain now than then. Gold, which is so often a dangerous *ignis fatuus*, did not appear to deceive them. But coal, which is much more desirable than gold, was reported by several, and once at least with reasonable certainty.

The boat that landed from Behring, when he discovered the coast, found among other things "a whetstone on which it appeared that copper knives had been sharpened." This was the first sign of that mineral wealth which already excites such an interest. At another point where Behring landed "one of the Americans had a knife hanging by his side, of which his people took notice on account of its unusual make." It has been supposed that this knife was of iron. Next came Cook, who, when in Prince William sound, saw "copper and iron." In his judgment the iron came through the intervention of Indian tribes from Hudson bay or the settlements on the Canadian lakes, and his editor refers in a note to the knife seen by Behring as coming from the same quarter; but Cook thought that the copper was obtained near at home, as the natives, when engaged in barter, gave the idea "that having so much of this metal of their own they wanted no more." Naturally enough, for they were not far from the Copper river. Maurelle, the French officer in the service of Spain, landed in sight of Mount St. Elias in 1779, and he reports Indians with arrow-heads of copper, "which made the Spaniards suspect mines of this metal there." La Pérouse, who was also in this neighborhood, after mentioning that the naturalists of the expedition allowed no rock or stone to escape observation, reports ochre, schist, mica, very pure quartz, granite, pyrites of copper, plumbago, and coal, and then adds that some things announce that the mountains contain mines of iron and copper. He reports further that the natives had daggers of iron and sometimes of red copper; that the latter metal was common enough with them, serving for ornaments and for the points of their arrows; and he then states the very question of Cook with regard to the way in which they acquired these metals. He insists that "the natives know how to forge iron and work copper." Spears and arrows 'pointed with bone or iron," and also "an iron dagger" for each man, appear in Vancouver's account of the natives on the parallel of 54° 59′, just within the southern limits of Russian America. Lisiansky also saw at Sitka 'a thin plate of virgin copper," found on Copper river, three feet in length and at one end twenty inches in breadth, with figures painted on its sides, which had come from the possession of the natives. Meares reports "pure malleable lumps of copper in the possession of the natives," sometimes weighing as much as a pound, also necklaces, all obtained in barter with other natives further north. Portlock, while in Cook's inlet, in latitude 59° 26′, at a place called Graham's harbor, makes another discovery. Walking round the bay he saw "two veins of Kennel coal just above the beach, and with very little trouble several pieces were got out of the bank nearly as large as a man's hand." If the good captain did not report more than he saw this would be most important, for from the time when the amusing biographer of Lord Keeper North described that clean flaky coal which he calls "candle," because often used for its light, but which is generally called Kennel, no coal has been more of a household favorite. He reports further that "returning on board in the evening he tried some of the coal, and found it to burn clear and well." Add to these different reports the general testimony of Meares, who, when dwelling on the resources of this country, boldly includes "mines which are known to be between the latitudes of 40° and 60° north, and which may

hereafter prove a most valuable source of commerce between America and China."

It is especially when we seek to estimate the mineral products that we feel the want of careful explorations. We know more of the roving aborigines than of these stationary citizens of the soil. We know more of the trees. A tree is conspicuous. A mineral is hidden in the earth, to be found by chance or science. Thus far it seems as if chance only had ruled. The Russian Government handed over the country to a trading company, whose exclusive interest was furs. The company only followed its business when it looked to wild beasts with rich skins rather than to the soil. Its mines were above ground, and not below. There were also essential difficulties in the way of any explorations. The interior was practically inaccessible. The thick forest, saturated with rain and overgrown with wet mosses, presented obstacles which nothing but enlightened enterprise could overcome. Even at a short distance from the port of Sitka all effort had failed, and the inner recesses of the island, only thirty miles broad, were never penetrated.

The late Professor Henry D. Rogers, in his admirable paper on the Physical Features of America, being a part of his contribution to Keith Johnston's Atlas, full of knowledge and of fine generalization, says of this northwest belt of country that it is "little known in its topography to any but the roving Indians and the thinly-scattered fur-trappers." But there are certain general features which he proceeds to designate. According to him it belongs to what is known as the tertiary period of geology, intervening between the cretaceous period and that now in progress, but including also granite, gneiss, and ancient metamorphic rocks. It is not known if the true coal measures prevail in any part, although there is reason to believe that they may exist on the coast of the Arctic ocean between Cape Lisburne and Point Barrow.

Beginning at the south we have Sitka and its associate islands, composed chiefly of volcanic rocks, with limestone near. Little is known even of the coast between Sitka and Mount St. Elias, which, itself a volcano, is the beginning of a volcanic region occupying the peninsula of Alaska and the Aleutian islands, and having no less than thirty volcanoes, some extinct, but others still active. Most of the rocks here are volcanic, and the only fossiliferous beds are of the tertiary period. North of Alaska, and near the mouth of the Kwichpak, the coast seems to be volcanic or metamorphic, and probably tertiary, with a vein of lignite near the head of Norton's sound. At the head of Kotzebue's sound the cliffs abound in the bones of elephants and other extinct mammals, together with those of the musk ox and animals now living in the same latitude. From Kotzebue's sound northward the coast has a volcanic character. Then at Cape Thompson it is called sub-carboniferous, followed by rocks of the carboniferous age, being limestones, shales, and sandstones, which extend from Cape Lisburne far round to Point Barrow. At Cape Beaufort, very near the seventieth parallel of latitude, and north of the Arctic Circle, on a high ridge a quarter of a mile from the beach is a seam of coal, which appears to be of the true coal measures.

From this general outline, which leaves much in uncertainty, I come now to what is more important.

It is not entirely certain that *Iron* has been found in this region, although frequently reported. The evidence points to the south, and also to the north. Near Sitka it was reported by the Russian engineer Doroschin, although it does not appear that anything has been done to verify his report. A visitor there as late as last year saw excellent iron, reported to be from a bed in the neighborhood, which was said to be inexhaustible, and with abundant wood for its reduction. Then again on Kotzebue's sound specimens have been collected. At 66° 35′ Kotzebue found a false return in his calculations, which he attributes to the disturbing influence of "iron." A resident on the Youkon thinks that there is iron in that neighborhood.

Silver also has been reported at Sitka by the same Russian engineer who reported iron there; and, like the iron, in "sufficient quantity to pay for the working."

Lead was reported by the Russian explorer, Lieutenant Zagoyskin, on the lower part of the Kwichpak; but it is not known to what extent it exists.

Copper is found on the banks of the Copper river, called by the natives Mjednaja, meaning copper, and of its affluent, the Tshitachitna, in masses sometimes as large as forty pounds. Of this there can be little doubt. It is mentioned by Golowin in the *Archiv* of Erman as late as 1868. It was undoubtedly from this neighborhood that the copper was obtained which arrested the attention of the early navigators. Traces of copper are also found in other places on the coast; also in the mountains near the Youkon, where the Indians use it for arrow-heads.

Coal seems to exist all along the coast; according to Golowin "everywhere in greater or less abundance." Traces of it are reported on the islands of the Sitkan archipelago, and this is extremely probable, for it has been worked successfully on Vancouver's island below. It is also found on the Kenaian peninsula, Alaska, the island of Unga, belonging to the Shumagin group, Ounalaska, and far to the north at Beaufort. At the latter place it is "slaty, burning with a pure flame and rapid consumption," and it is supposed that there are extensive beds in the neighborhood better in quality. For an account of this coal I refer to the scientific illustrations of Beechey's Voyage. The natives also report coal in the interior on the Kwichpak. The coal of Ounalaska and probably of Alaska is tertiary and not adapted for steamers. With regard to that of Unga scientific authorities are divided. That of the Kenaian peninsula is the best and the most extensive. It is found on the eastern side of Cook's inlet, half way between Cape Anchor and the Russian settlement of St. Nicholas, in veins three quarters of a yard or more in thickness, and ranging in quality from mere carboniferous wood to anthracite. According to one authority these coal veins extend and spread themselves far in the interior. It appears that this coal has been more than once sent to California for trial, and that it was there pronounced a good article. Since then it has been mined by the company, not only for their own uses, but also for export to California. In making these statements I rely particularly upon Golowin in the *Archiv* of Erman, and also upon the elaborate work of Grewingk, in the Transactions of the Mineralogical Society of Petersburg for 1848 and 1849, (p. 112,) where will be found a special map of the Kenaian peninsula.

Gold is less important than coal, but its discovery produces more excitement. The report of gold in any quarter stimulates the emigrant or the adventurer who hopes to obtain riches swiftly. Nor is this distant region without such experience. Only a few years ago the British colony of Victoria was aroused by a rumor of gold in the mountains of the Stikine river, not far in the interior from Sitka. At once there was a race that way, and the solitudes of this river were penetrated by hunters in quest of the glittering ore. Discomfiture ensued. Gold had been found, but not in any sufficient quantities reasonably accessible. Nature for the present set up obstacles. But failure in one place will be no discouragement in another, especially as there is reason to believe that the mountains here contain a continuation of those auriferous deposits which have become so famous further south. The Sierra Nevada chain of California reaches here.

Traces of gold have been observed at other points. One report places a deposit not far from Sitka. The same writer, who reports iron there, also reports that during the last year he saw a piece of gold as large as a marble, which was shown by an Indian. But the Russian engineer, Doroschin, furnishes testimony more precise. He reports gold in at least three different localities, each of considerable extent. The first is the mountain range on the north of Cook's inlet and extending into Alaska, consisting principally of clay slate with permeating veins of Diorite, the latter being known as a gold-bearing rock. He observed this in the summer of 1851. About the same time certain Indians from the Bay of Jakutat, not far from Mount St. Elias, brought him specimens of Diorite found in their neighborhood, making, therefore, a second deposit. In the summer of 1855 the same engineer found gold on the southern side of Cook's inlet, in the mountains of the Kenay peninsula. Satisfying himself, first, that the bank occupied by the redoubt of St. Nicholas, at the mouth of the Kaknu river, is gold-bearing, he was induced to fellow the development of Diorite in the upper valley of the river, and as he ascended found a gold-bearing alluvion gradually increasing, with scales of gold becoming coarser and coarser, instead of being scarcely visible as at first.

It does not appear that the discoveries on Cook's inlet were pursued; but it is reported that the Hudson Bay Company, holding the country about the Bay of Jakutat under a lease from the Russian company, have found the Diorite in that neighborhood valuable. This incident has given rise to a recent controversy. Russian journals attacked the engineer for remissness in not exploring the Jakutat country. He has defended himself by setting out what he actually did in the way of discovery, and the essential difficulty at the time in doing more; all which will be found in a number just received of the work to which I have so often referred, the *Archiv von Russland* by Erman for 1866, volume 25, page 229.

Thus much for the mineral resources of this new-found country as they have been recognized at a few points on the extensive coast, leaving the vast unknown interior without a word.

Furs.

VI. I pass now to *Furs*, which at times have vied with minerals in value, although the supply is more limited and less permanent. Trappers are "miners" of the forest, seeking furs as others seek gold. The parallel continues also in the greed and oppression unhappily incident to the pursuit. A Russian officer who was one of the early visitors to this coast remarks that to his mind the only prospect of relief for the suffering natives "consists in the total extirpation of the animals of the chase," which he thought from the daily havoc must take place in a very few years. This was at the close of the last century. The trade still continues, though essentially diminished, an important branch of commerce.

Early in this commerce desirable furs were obtained in barter for a trifle, and when something of value was exchanged it was much out of proportion to the furs. This has been the case generally in dealing with the natives, until their eyes have been slowly opened. In Kamtschatka, at the beginning of the last century, half a dozen sables were obtained in exchange for a knife, and a dozen for a hatchet; and the Kamtschatkadales wondered that their Cossack conquerors were willing to pay so largely for what seemed worth so little. Similar incidents on the northwest coast are reported by the early navigators. Cook mentions that in exchange for "beads" the Indians at Prince William sound "gave whatever they had, even their fine sea otter skins," which they prized no more than other skins, until it appeared how much they were prized by their visitors. Where there was no competition prices rose slowly, and many years after Cook the Russians at Kodiak, "in return for trinkets and tobacco," received twelve sea otter skins and fox skins of different kinds to the number of

near six hundred. These instances will show in a general way the spirit of this trade even to our own day. On the coast, and especially in the neighborhood of the factories, the difference in the value of furs is recognized, and a proportionate price is obtained, which Sir Edward Belcher found in 1837 to be "for a moderately good sea otter skin from six to seven blankets, increasing to thirteen for the best, together with sundry knickknacks." But in the interior it is otherwise. A recent resident in the region of the Youkon assures me that he has seen skins worth several hundred dollars bartered for goods worth only fifty cents.

Beside whalers and casual ships with which the Esquimaux are in the habit of dealing, the commerce in furs on both sides of the continent north of the United States has for a long time been in the hands of two corporations, being the Hudson Bay Company, with its directors in London, and the Russian American Company, with its directors in St. Petersburg. The former is much the older of the two, and has been the most flourishing. Its original members were none other than Prince Rupert, the Duke of Albemarle, Earl Craven, Lord Ashley, and other eminent associates, who received a charter from Charles II in 1670 to prosecute a search after a new passage to the South sea and to establish a trade in furs, minerals, and other considerable commodities in all those seas and in the British possessions north and west of Canada, with powers of government, the whole constituting a colossal monopoly, which stretched from Labrador and Baffin bay to an undefined west. At present this great corporation is known only as a fur company, to which all its powers are tributary. For some time its profits have been so considerable that it has been deemed advisable to hide them by nominal additions to the stock. With the extinction of the St. Petersburg corporation under the present treaty the London corporation will remain the only existing fur company on the continent, but necessarily restrained in its operation to British territory. It remains to be seen into whose hands the commerce on the Pacific side will fall now that this whole region will be open to the unchecked enterprise of our citizens.

This remarkable commerce began before the organization of the company. Its profits may be inferred from a voyage in 1772, described by Coxe, between Kamtschatka and the Aleutians. The tenth part of the skins being handed to the custom-house, the remainder was distributed in fifty-five shares, containing each twenty sea otters, sixteen black and brown foxes, ten red foxes, three sea otter tails, and these shares were sold on the spot at from eight hundred to one thousand rubles each, so that the whole lading brought about fifty thousand rubles. The cost of these may be inferred from the articles given in exchange. A Russian outfit, of which I find a contemporary record, was, among other things, "seven hundred weight of tobacco; one hundred weight of glass beads; perhaps a dozen spare hatchets and a few superfluous knives, of very bad quality; an immense number of traps for foxes; a few hams; a little rancid butter." With such imports against such exports the profits must have been considerable.

From Langsdorf we have a general inventory of the furs at the beginning of the century in the principal magazine of the Russian company on the island of Kodiak, collected on the islands, the peninsula of Alaska, Cook's inlet, Prince William sound, and the continent generally. Here were "a great variety of the rarest kinds of fox skins," black, blackish, reddish, silver gray, and stone fox, the latter probably a species of the Arctic; brown and red bears, "the skins of which are of great value," and also "the valuable black bear;" the zisel marmot and the common marmot; the glutton; the lynx, chiefly of whitish gray; the reindeer; the beaver; the hairy hedgehog; the wool of a wild American sheep, whitish, fine, and very long, but he could never obtain sight of the animal that produced this wool; also "sea otters, once the principal source of wealth to the company, now nearly extirpated, a few hundreds only being annually collected." The same furs were reported by Cook as found on this coast in his day, including even the wild sheep. They all continue to be found, except that I hear nothing of any wild sheep save at a Sitkan dinner.

There has been much exaggeration with regard to the profits of the Russian corporation. An English writer of authority calls them "immense," and adds that formerly they were much greater. I refer to the paper of Mr. Petermann, read before the Geographical Society of London in 1852. (Journal, vol. 22, p. 120.) · The number of skins reported at times is prodigious, although this fails to reveal precisely the profits. For instance, Pribolow collected within two years on the islands north of Alaska, which bear his name, the skins of 2,000 sea otters, 6,000 dark ice foxes, 40,000 sea bears or ursine seals, together with 1,000 poods of walrus ivory. The pood is a Russian weight of thirty-six pounds. Lütke mentions that in 1803 no less than 800,000 skins of the ursine seal were accumulated in the factory at Ounalaska, of which 700,000 were thrown into the sea, partly because they were badly prepared and partly in order to keep up the price, thus imitating the Dutch, who for the same reason burnt their spices. Another estimate masses the collection for a series of years. From 1787 to 1817, for only a part of which time the company existed, the Ounalaska district yielded upwards of 2,500,000 seal skins; and from 1817 to 1838, during all which time the company was in power, the same district yielded 579,000 seal skins. Assuming what is improbable, that these skins were sold at twenty-five rubles each, some calculating genius has ciphered out the sum-total of proceeds at more than eighty-five million rubles; or, calling the ruble seventy-five cents, a sum-total of more than sixty-three

million dollars. Clearly the latter years can show no approximation to any such doubtful result.

Descending from these lofty figures, which if not exaggerations are at least generalities and relate partly to the earlier periods, before the time of the company, we shall have a better idea of the commerce if we look at authentic reports for special periods of time. Admiral Von Wrangel, who was for so long governor, must have been well informed. According to statements in his work, adopted also by Wappäus in his *Geographie*, the company from 1826 to 1833, a period of seven years, exported the skins of the following animals: 9,853 sea otters, with 8,751 sea otter tails, 40,000 river beavers, 6,242 river or land otters, 5,243 black foxes, 7,759 black bellied foxes, 1,633 red foxes, 24,000 polar foxes, 1,093 lynxes, 559 wolverines, 2,976 sables, 4,335 swamp otters, 69 wolves, 1,261 bears, 505 muskrats, 132,160 seals, 830 poods of whalebone, 1,490 poods of walrus ivory, and 7,122 sacks of castoreum. What was their value does not appear. Sir George Simpson, the governor-in-chief of the Hudson Bay Company, who was at Sitka in 1841, represents the returns of the company for that year as follows: 10,000 fur seals, 1,000 sea otters, 2,500 land otters, and 20,000 walrus teeth, without including foxes and martens. There is still one other report for the year 1852, as follows: 1,231 sea otters, 129 young sea otters, 2,948 common otters, 14,486 fur seals, 107 bears, 13,300 beavers, 2 wolves, 458 sables, 243 lynxes, 163 moleskins, 1,504 bags of castoreum, 684 black foxes, 1,590 cross foxes, 5,174 red foxes, 2,359 blue Arctic foxes, 355 white Arctic foxes, and also 31 foxes called white, perhaps Albinos.

Besides these reports for special years, I am enabled to present from the Russian tables of Captain Golowin another, covering the period from 1842 to 1860, inclusive, being as follows: 25,602 sea otters, 63,826 "otters," probably river otters, 161,042 beavers, 73,944 foxes, 55,540 Arctic foxes, 2,283 bears, 6,445 lynxes, 26,384 sables, 19,076 muskrats, 2,536 ursine seals, 338,604 marsh otters, 712 "pairs of hare," 451 martens, 104 wolves, 46,274 castoreums, 7,309 beavers' tails. Here is an inexplicable absence of seal skins. On the other hand, sables, which belong to Asia and not to America, are mentioned. The list is Russian; and perhaps embraces furs from the Asiatic islands of the company.

From a competent source I learn that the value of skins at Sitka during the last year was substantially as follows: sea otter, $50; marten, $4; beaver, $2 50; bear, $4 50; black fox, $50; silver fox, $40; cross fox, $25; red fox, $2. A recent Price Current in New York gives the prices there in currency, as follows: silver fox, $10 to $50; cross fox, $3 to $5; red fox $1 to $1 50; otter, $3 to $6; mink, $3 to $6; beaver, $1 to $4; muskrat, twenty to fifty cents; lynx, $2 to $4; black bear, $6 to $12; dark marten, $5 to $20. These New York prices vary from those of Sitka. The latter will be the better guide to a comprehension of the proceeds at Sitka, which of course must be subject to deduction for the expenses of the company. Of the latter I say nothing now as I have considered them in speaking of the existing government.

The skins, it appears, are obtained in three different ways: first, through the hunters employed by the company; secondly, in payment of taxes imposed by the company; and thirdly, by barter or purchase from independent natives. But with all these sources it is certain that the Russian company has enjoyed no success comparable to that of its British rival; and still more, there is reason to believe that latterly its profits have not been large.

Amid all the concealment or obscurity which prevails with regard to the revenues of the company, it is easy to see that for some time there must be a large amount of valuable furs on this coast. The bountiful solitudes of the forest and of the adjoining waters have not yet been exhausted; nor will they be until civilization has supplied substitutes. Such, indeed, is a part of that humane law of compensation which contributes so much to the general harmony. For the present there will be trappers on the land, who will turn aside only a little from its prizes there to obtain from the sea its otter, seal, and walrus. It cannot be irrelevant, and may not be without interest, if I call your attention briefly to those fur-bearing animals, which are about to be brought within the sphere of republican government. If we cannot find their exact census we may at least learn something of their character and value.

The comparative poverty of vegetation in the more northern parts of the continent contrasts with the abundance of animal life, especially if we embrace those tenants of the sea who seek the land for rest. These northern parallels are hardly less productive than the tropics. The lion, the elephant, and the hippopotamus find their counterpart in the bear, the walrus, and the seal, without including the sables and the foxes. Here again nature by an unerring law adapts the animal to the climate, and in providing him with needful protection creates also a needful supply for the protection of man; and this is the secret of rich furs. Under the sun of the tropics such provision is as little needed by man as by beast, and therefore nature, which does nothing inconsistent with a wise economy, reserves it for other places. .

Among the furs most abundant in this commerce are those of the Fox, in its different species and under its different names. Its numbers were noticed very early, and gave the name to the eastern group of the Aleutians, which were called Lyssie Ostrowa, or Fox islands. Some of its furs are among the very precious. The most plentiful is the Red, or as it is sometimes called American; but this fur is not highly prized. Then comes the Arctic, of little value, and of different colors, sometimes blue, and in full winter dress pure white, whose circumpolar home is indicated by his name. The Cross Fox is less known, but much more sought from the fineness of its fur and its color. Its name is derived from dark cruciform stripes, extending from the head to the back and at right angles over the shoulders. It is now recognized to be a variety of the red, from which it differs more in commercial value than in general character. The Black Fox, which is sometimes entirely of shining black with silver white at the tip of the tail, is called also the Silver Fox, when the black hairs of the body are tipped with white. They are of the same name in science, sometimes called Argentatus, although there seem to be two different names, if not different values, in commerce. This variety is more rare than the Cross Fox. Not more than four or five are taken during a season at any one post in the fur countries, although the hunters use every art for this purpose. The temptation is great, as we are told that "its fur fetches six times the price of any other fur produced in North America." Sir John Richardson, who is the authority for this statement, forgot the Sea Otter, of which he seems to have known little. Without doubt the Black Fox is admired for its rarity and beauty. La Hontan, the French commander in Canada under Louis XIV, speaks of its fur in his time as worth its weight in gold.

Among the animals whose furs are less regarded are the Wolverine, known in science as gulo or glutton, and called by Buffon the quadruped vulture, with a dark-brown fur, which becomes black in winter, and resembles that of the bear, but is not so long nor of so much value. There is also the Lynx, belonging to the feline race, living north of the great lakes and eastward of the Rocky mountains, with a fur moderately prized in commerce. There is also the Muskrat, which is abundant in Russian America, as it is common on this continent, whose fur enters largely into the cheaper peltries of the United States in so many different ways, and with such various artificial colors, that the animal would not know his own skin.

Among inferior furs I may include that very respectable animal, the Black Bear, reported by Cook "in great numbers and of a shiny black color." The Grizzly Bear is less frequent and is inferior in quality of fur to all the varieties of the bear. The Brown Bear is supposed to be a variety of the Black Bear. The Polar Bear, which at times is a formidable animal, leaving a foot-print in the snow nine inches long, was once said not to make an appearance west of the Mackenzie river, but he has been latterly found on Behring straits, so that he, too, is included among our new population. The Black Bear, in himself a whole population, inhabits every wooded district from the Atlantic to the Pacific, and from Carolina to the ice of the Arctic, becoming more numerous inland than on the coast. Langsdorf early remarked that he did not appear on the Aleutians, but on the continent, near Cook's inlet and Prince William sound, which are well wooded. He has been found even on the isthmus of Panama. Next to the dog he is the most cosmopolitan and perhaps the most intelligent of animals, and among those of the forest he is the most known, even to the nursery. His showy fur once enjoyed great vogue in hammercloths and muffs, and it is still used in military caps and pistol holsters; so that he is sometimes called the Army Bear. Latterly the fur has .fallen in value. Once it brought in London from twenty to forty guineas. It will now hardly bring more than that same number of shillings.

The *Beaver*, amphibious and intelligent, has a considerable place in commerce, and also a notoriety of its own as the familiar synonym for the common covering of a man's head, and here the animal becomes historic.. By royal proclamation in 1638 Charles I of England prohibited the use of any material in the manufacture of hats "except beaver stuff or beaver wool." This proclamation was the death warrant of beavers innumerable, sacrificed to the demands of the trade. Wherever they existed over a wide extent of country, in the shelter of forests or in lodges built by their extraordinary instinct, they were pursued and arrested in their busy work. The importation of their skins into Europe during the last century was enormous, and it continued until one year it is said to have reached the unaccountable number of six hundred thousand. I give these figures as I find them. Latterly other materials have been obtained for hats, so that this fur has become less valuable. But the animal is still hunted. A medicine supplied by him, and known as the *Castoreum*, has a fixed place in the Materia Medica.

The *Marten* is perhaps the most popular of all the fur-bearing animals that belong to our new possessions. An inhabitant of the whole wooded region of the continent, he finds a favorite home in the cold forests of the Youkon, where he needs his beautiful fur, which is not much inferior to that of his near relative, the far-famed Russian sable. In the trade of the Hudson Bay Company the Marten occupies the largest place, his skins for a single district amounting to more than fifty thousand annually, and being sometimes sold as sable. The Ermine, which is of the same Weasel family, is of little value except for its captivating name, although its fur finds its way to the English market in enormous quantities. The Mink, also of the same general family, was once little regarded, but now, by a freak of fashion in our country, this animal has ascended in value above the Beaver, and almost to the level of the Marten. His fur is plentiful on the Youkon and along the coast. Specimens in the Museum of the Smithsonian Institution attest its occurrence at Sitka.

The *Seal*, amphibious, polygamous, and intelligent as the beaver, has always supplied the largest multitude of furs to the Russian Company. The early navigators describe its appearance and numbers. Cook encountered them constantly. Excellent swimmers, ready divers, they seek rocks and recesses for repose, where, though watchful and never sleeping long without moving, they become the prey of the hunter. Early in the century there was a wasteful destruction of them. Young and old, male and female, were indiscriminately knocked on the head for the sake of their skins. Sir George Simpson, who saw this improvidence with an experienced eye, says that it was hurtful in two ways: first, the race was almost exterminated; and secondly, the market was glutted sometimes with as many as two hundred thousand a year, so that prices did not pay the expense of carriage. The Russians were led to adopt the plan of the Hudson Bay Company, killing only a limited number of males who have attained their full growth, which can be done easily, from the known and systematic habits of the animal. Under this economy seals have multiplied again, vastly increasing the supply.

Besides the common seal there are various species, differing in appearance, so as to justify different names, and yet all with a family character, including the sea leopard, so named from his spots; the elephant seal, from his tusks and proboscis; and the sea lion, with teeth, mane, and a thick cylindrical body. These are of little value, although their skins are occasionally employed. The skin of the elephant seal is strong, so as to justify its use in the harness of horses. There is also the sea bear, or *Ursine Seal*, very numerous in these waters, whose skin, especially if young, is prized for clothing. Steller speaks with grateful remembrance of a garment which he made from one while on the desert island after the shipwreck of Behring.

Associated with the seal, and belonging to the same family, is the *Walrus*, called by the British the sea-horse, the morse or the sea-cow, and by the French *Bête à la Grande Dent*. His two tusks, rather than his skin, are the prize of the hunter. Unlike the rest of the seal family, he is monogamous and not polygamous. Cook vividly describes an immense herd asleep on the ice, with one of their number on guard, and when aroused roaring and baying aloud, while they huddled and tumbled together like swine. At times their multitude is so great that before being aroused several hundreds are slaughtered, as game in a park. Their hide is excellent for carriage braces, and is useful about ship. But it is exclusively for their ivory that these hecatombs are sacrificed. A single tooth weighs sometimes several pounds. Twenty thousand teeth reported as an annual harvest of the Russian Company must cost the lives of ten thousand walruses. The ivory compares with that of the elephant, and is for some purposes superior. Long ago, in the days of Saxon history, a Norwegian at the court of Alfred exhibited to the king "teeth of price and excellency" from what he called a horse whale. Unquestionably these were teeth of walrus.

I mention the *Sea Otter* last; but in beauty and value it is the first. In these respects it far surpasses the river or land otter, which though beautiful and valuable must yield the palm. It has also more the manners of the seal, with its fondness for sea-washed rocks, and with a maternal affection almost human. The Sea Otter seems to belong exclusively to the rorlh Pacific. Its haunts once extended as far as the bay of San Francisco; but long ago it ceased to appear in that southern region. Cook saw it at Nootka sound. Vancouver reports it at Chatham strait "in immense numbers, so that it was easily in the power of the natives to procure as many as they chose to be at the trouble of taking." But these navigators, could they revisit this coast, would not find it in these places now. Its present zone is between the parallels of 60° and 65° north latitude on the American and Asiatic coasts, so that its range is very limited. Evidently it was Cook who first revealed the Sea Otter to Englishmen. In the table of contents of his third voyage are the words, *Description of the Sea Otter;* and in the pages that follow there is a minute account of this animal, and especially of its incomparable fur, which is pronounced "certainly softer and finer than that of any other we know of." Not content with description the famous navigator adds in remarkable words, "therefore, the discovery of this part of North America, where so valuable an article of commerce may be met with, cannot be a matter of indifference." These words stimulated the commercial enterprise of that day. Other witnesses followed. Meares, describing his voyage to this coast, placed this fur high above all other furs; "the finest in the world, and of exceeding beauty," and La Pérouse made it known in France as "peltry the most precious and common in those seas." Shortly afterwards all existing information with regard to it was elaborately set forth in the Historical Introduction to the Voyages of Marchand, published at Paris under the auspices of the Institute.

The Sea Otter was known originally to the Russians in Kamtschatka, where it was called the sea beaver; but the discoveries of Behring constitute an epoch in the commerce. His shipwrecked crew, compelled to winter on the desert island which now bears his name, found this animal in flocks, ignorant of men and innocent as sheep, so that they were slaughtered without resistance to the number of more than eight hundred. Their value became known. Fabulous prices were paid by the Chinese, sometimes, according to Coxe, as high as one hundred and forty rubles. At such a price a single Sea Otter was more than an ounce of gold, and a flock was a gold mine. The pursuit of gold was renewed. It was the Sea Otter that tempted the navigator, and subsequent discovery was under the incentive of obtaining the precious fur. Müller, calling him a beaver, says in his history of Russian Discovery, "the catching of beavers enticed many people to go to these parts, and they never returned without great quantities, which always produced large prices." All that could be obtained were sent to China, which was the objective point commercially for this whole coast. The trade became a fury. Wherever the animal with exquisite purple-black fur appeared he was killed; not always without effort, for he had learned something of his huntsman and was now coy and watchful, so that his pursuit was often an effort, but his capture was always a triumph. The natives, who had been accustomed to his furs as clothing, surrendered them. Sometimes a few beads were their only pay. All the navigators speak of the unequal barter. "Any sort of beads" were enough, according to Cook. The story is best told by Meares who says "such as were dressed in furs instantly stripped themselves, and in return for a moderate quantity of spike nails we received sixty-five sea otter skins." Vancouver describes the "humble fashion" of the natives in poor skins as a substitute for the beautiful furs appropriated by their "Russian friends." The picture is completed by the Russian navigator when he confesses that "after the Russians had any intercourse with them" the natives ceased to wear Sea Otter skins. In the growing rage the Sea Otter nearly disappeared. Langsdorf reports them as "nearly extirpated, since the high prices for them induces the Russians for a momentary advantage to kill all they meet with, both old and young. Nor can they see that by such a procedure they must soon be deprived of the trade entirely." This was in 1804. Since then the indiscriminate massacre has been arrested.

Meanwhile our countrymen entered into this commerce, so that Russians, Englishmen, and Americans were all engaged in slaughtering Sea Otters and selling their furs to the Chinese until the market of Canton was glutted. Lisiansky, on his arrival there, found "immense quantities in American ships." By and by the commerce was engrossed by the Russians and English. And now it passes into the hands of the United States with all the other prerogatives belonging to this territory.

Fisheries.

VII. I come now to the *Fisheries*, the last head of this inquiry, and not inferior to any other in importance; perhaps the most important of all. What even are Sea Otter skins by the side of that product of the sea, incalculable in amount, which contributes to the sustenance of the human family?

Here, as elsewhere, in the endeavor to estimate the resources of this region, there is vagueness and uncertainty. Information at least is wanting; and yet we are not entirely ignorant. Nothing is clearer than that fish in great abundance are taken everywhere on the coast, around the islands, in the bays, and throughout the adjacent seas. On this head the evidence is constant and complete. Here are oysters, clams, crabs, and a dainty little fish of the herring tribe called the oolachan, contributing to the luxury of the table, and so rich in its oily nature that the natives are said to use it sometimes as a "candle." Besides these, which I name now only to put aside, are those great staples of commerce and mainstays of daily subsistence, the Salmon, the Herring, the Halibut, the Cod, and behind all the Whale. This short list is enough, for it offers a constant feast, with the Whale at hand for light. Here is the best that the sea affords for the poor or the rich; for daily use or for the fast days of the church. Here also is a sure support at least to the inhabitants of the coast.

But in order to determine the value of this supply we must go further and ascertain if these various tribes of fish, reputed to be in such numbers, are found under such conditions and in such places as to constitute a permanent and profitable Fishery. This is the practical question, which is still undecided. It will not be enough to show that the whole coast may be subsisted by its fish. It should be shown further that the fish of this coast can be made to subsist other places, so as to become a valuable article of commerce. And here uncertainty begins. The proper conditions of an extensive Fishery are not yet understood. It is known that certain Fisheries exist in certain waters and on certain soundings, but the spaces of ocean are obscure, even to the penetrating eye of science. Fishing banks known for ages are still in many respects a mystery, which is increased where the Fishery is recent or only coastwise. There are other banks, which fail from local incidents. Thus very lately a Cod Fishery was commenced on Rochdale bank, sixty-five miles northwest of the Hebrides; but the deep rolling of the Atlantic and the intolerable weather compelled its abandonment.

Before proceeding to consider the capacity of this region for an extensive Fishery it is important to know such evidence as exists with regard to the supply, and here again we must resort to the early navigators and visitors. Their evidence, reënforced by modern reports, is an essential element, even if it does not entirely determine the question.

Down to the arrival of Europeans on this coast the natives lived on fish. This had been their constant food, with small additions from the wild vegetation of the country. In summer it was fish freshly caught; in winter it was fish dried or preserved. At the first landing on the discovery Steller found in the deserted cellar which he visited "store of red salmon," and the sailors brought away "smoked fishes" that appeared like carp and tasted very well." This is the earliest notice of fish on this coast, which are thus directly associated with its discovery. The next of interest which appears is the account of a Russian navigator in 1765, who reports on the Fox islands, and especially Oonalaska, "Cod, perch, pilchards, smelts." Thus early Cod appears.

If we repair to Cook's Voyages we shall find the accustomed instruction, and here I shall quote with all possible brevity. At Nootka sound he reports fish "more plentiful than birds," of which the principal sorts in great numbers were "the common Herring, but scarcely exceeding seven inches in length, and a smaller sort, the same with the anchovy or sardine," and now and then "a small brownish Cod, spotted with white." Then again, he reports at the same place "Herrings and sardines and small Cod," the former "not only eaten fresh, but likewise dried and smoked." In Prince William sound he reports that "the only fish got were some torsk and Halibut, chiefly brought by the natives to sell." Near Kodiak he reports that "having three hours calm his people caught upward of a hundred Halibuts, some of which weighed a hundred pounds, and none less than twenty pounds," and he adds, naturally enough, "a very seasonable refreshment." In Bristol bay, on the northern side of Alaska, he reports "tolerable success in fishing, catching Cod, and now and then a few flat-fish." In Norton sound, still further north, he reports that in exchange for four knives made from an old iron hoop he obtained of the natives "near four hundred pounds weight of fish caught on this or the preceding day; some trout, and the rest in size and taste between the mullet and a Herring." On his return southward, stopping at Oonalaska, he reports "plenty of fish, at first mostly Salmon, both fresh and dried; some of the salmon in high perfection; also salmon, trout, and once a Halibut that weighed two hundred and fifty-four pounds;" and in describing the habits of the islanders he reports that "they dry large quantities of fish in summer, which they lay up in small huts for winter's use." Such is the testimony of Captain Cook.

No experience on the coast is more instructive than that of Portlock, and from his report I compile a succinct diary. July 20, 1786, at Graham's harbor, Cook's inlet: "The Russian chief brought me as a present a quantity of fine Salmon, sufficient to serve both ships for one day." July 21: "In several hauls caught about thirty Salmon and a few flat-fish;" also further, "The Russian settlement had on one side a small lake of fresh water, on which plenty of fine Salmon were caught." July 22: "The boat returned deeply loaded with fine Salmon." July 28, latitude 60° 09′: "Two small canoes came off; they had nothing to barter but a few dried Salmon." July 30: "Plenty of excellent fresh Salmon obtained for beads and buttons." August 3: "Plenty of fine Salmon." August 9, at Cook's inlet: "The greatest abundance of fine Salmon." August 13: "Hereabouts would be most desirable situation for carrying on a Whale Fishery, the whales being on the coast and close in shore in vast numbers, and there being convenient and excellent harbors quite handy for the business." After these entries the English navigator left the coast for the Sandwich islands.

Returning during the next year, Portlock continued to record his observations, which I abstract in brief. May 21, 1787. Port Etches, latitude 60° 21': "The harbor affords very fine crabs and muscles." June 4: "A few Indians came alongside, bringing some *Halibut and Cod.*" June 20: "Plenty of flounders, crabs also plenty and fine. Several fishing alongside for flounders caught *Cod and Halibut.*" June 22: "Sent the canoe out some distance in the bay, and it soon returned with a *fine load of Cod and Halibut.* This induced me to send her out frequently with a fishing party, and they caught considerably more than was sufficient for daily consumption." June 30: "In hauling the seine caught a large quantity of *Herrings and some Salmon*; the Herrings, though small, were very good, and *two hogsheads of them were salted for sea store.*" July 7: "We daily caught *large quantities of Salmon*, but, the unsettled state of the weather not permitting us to cure them on board, sent the boatswain with a party on shore to build a house to smoke them in." July 11: "The seine was frequently hauled, and *not less than two thousand Salmon caught at each haul.* The weather, however, preventing us from curing them as well as could have been wished, we kept only a sufficient quantity for present use and let the rest escape. The Salmon were now in such numbers along the shores that any quantity whatever might be caught with the greatest ease." All this testimony of the English navigator is singularly explicit, while it is, in complete harmony with that of the Russian visitors and of Cook, who preceded.

The report of Meares is similar, although less minute. Speaking of the natives generally he says "they live entirely upon fish, but of all others they prefer the Whale." Then again, going into more detail, he says "vast quantities of fish are to be found, both on the coast, and in the sounds or harbors. Among these are the *Halibut, Herring,* sardine, silver-beam, salmon, trout, *Cod,* all of which we have seen in the possession of the natives, or have been caught by ourselves." The *Herrings* he describes as taken in such numbers "that a whole village has not been able to cleanse them." At Nootka the *Salmon* was of a very delicate flavor, and "the *Cod* taken by the natives of the best quality." French testimony is not wanting, although it is less precise. The early navigator, who was on the coast in 1779, remarks that "the fish most abundant is the *Salmon.*" La Pérouse, who was there in 1787, mentions a large fish weighing sometimes more than a hundred pounds, and several other fish, but he preferred "the *Salmon and Trout*, which the Indians sold in larger numbers than could be consumed." A similar report was made by Marchand, the other French navigator, who finds the sea and rivers abounding in "excellent fish," particularly *Salmon and Trout.*

Afterwards came the Russian navigator Billings in 1792; and here we have a similar report, only different in form. Describing the natives of Ounalaska the book in which this visit is recorded says "they *dry Salmon, Cod, and Halibut* for a winter supply." At Kodiak it says "Whales are in amazing numbers about the straits of the islands and in the vicinity of Kodiak." Then again the reporter, who was the naturalist Sauer, says "I observed the same species of *Salmon* here as at Okhotsk, and saw crabs." Then again, "the *Halibuts* in these seas are extremely large, some weighing seventeen poods, or six hundred and twelve pounds avoirdupois. The liver of this fish, as also of *Cod,* the natives deem unhealthy and never eat, but extract the oil from them." Then again, returning to Ounalaska, the reporter says "the other fish are *Halibut, Cod, two or three species of Salmon,* and sometimes one very common in Kamtschatka between four and five feet long."

From Lisiansky, another Russian navigator, who was on the coast in 1804, I take two passages. The first relates to the fish of Sitka. "For some time," he says, "we had been able to catch no fish but the *Halibut.* Those of the species which we caught were fine, some weighing eighteen stone, and were of an excellent flavor. This fish abounds here from March to November, when it retires from the coast till the winter is at an end." The other passage relates to the subsistence of the inhabitants during the winter. "They live," he says, "on *dried Salmon,* train oil, and the spawn of fish, especially that of *Herrings,* of which they always lay in a good stock."

Langsdorf, who was there at the same time, is more full and explicit. Of Ounalaska he says, "The principle food consists of fish, sea dogs, and the flesh of whales. Among the fish the most common and most abundant are several sorts of *Salmon, Cod, Herrings,* and *Holybutt.* The holybutts, which are the sort held in the highest esteem, are sometimes of an enormous size, weighing even several hundred pounds." Then again of Kodiak he says, "the most common fish, those which *fresh and dry* constitute a principal article of food, are *Herrings, Cod, Holybutt,* and *several sorts of Salmon*; the latter are taken in *prodigious numbers* by means of nets or dams." Of Sitka he says, "we have several sorts of *Salmon, Holybutt,* whitings, *Cod, and Herrings.*" A goodly variety.

Lütke, also a Russian, tells us that he found fish the standing dish at Sitka from the humblest servant to the governor, and he mentions *Salmon, Herrings, Cod,* and Turbot. Of Salmon there are no less than four kinds, which were eaten fresh when possible, but after June they were sent to the fortress salted. The Herrings appeared in February and March. The Cod and Turbot were caught in the straits during winter. Lütke also reports "fresh Cod" at Kodiak.

I close this abstract of foreign testimony by two English authorities often quoted. Sir Edward Belcher, while on this coast in 1837, records that "fish, *Halibut,* and *Salmon* of two kinds were abundant and moderate, of which the crews purchased and cured great quantities." Sir George Simpson, who was at Sitka in 1841, says "*Halibut, Cod, Herrings,* flounders, and many other sorts of fish are always to be had for the taking in unlimited quantities. Salmon have been known literally to embarrass the movements of a canoe. About one hundred thousand of this fish, equivalent to fifteen hundred barrels, are annually salted for the use of the establishment." Nothing could be stronger as statement, and when we consider the character of its author nothing could be stronger as authority.

Cumulative upon all this accumulation of testimony is that of recent visitors. Nobody visits this coast without testifying. The fish are so demonstrative in their abundance that all remark it. Officers of the United States Navy report the same fish substantially which Cook reported as far north as the Frozen ocean. Scientific explorers, prompted by the Smithsonian Institution, report Cod in Behring straits, on the limits of the Arctic Circle. One of these reports, that while anchored near Ounimak in 1865 the ship, with a couple of lines, caught "a great many fine Cod, most of them between two and three feet in length." He supposes that there is no place on the coast where they are not numerous. A citizen of Massachusetts, who has recently returned from a prolonged residence on this coast, writes me from Boston, under date of March 8, 1867, that "the Whale and Cod fisheries of the north Pacific are destined to form a very important element in the wealth of California and Washington Territory, and that already numbers of fishermen are engaged there and more are intending to leave." From all this testimony there can be but one conclusion with regard at least to certain kinds of fish.

Salmon exist in unequaled numbers, so that this fish, so aristocratic elsewhere, becomes common enough. Not merely the prize of epicures, it is the food of all. Not merely the pastime of gentle natures, like Isaac Walton or Humphrey Davy, who employ in its pursuit an elegant leisure, its capture is the daily reward of the humblest. On Vancouver's island it is the constant ration given out by the Hudson Bay Company to the men in their service. At Sitka ships are supplied with it gratuitously by the natives. By the side of the incalculable multitudes swarming out of the Arctic waters, haunting this extended coast, and peopling its rivers, so that at a single haul Portlock took not less than two thousand, how small an allowance are the two hundred thousand which the Salmon Fisheries of England annually supply.

Herring seem to be not less multitudinous than the Salmon. Their name, derived from the German *heer*, signifying an army, is amply verified. As on the coast of Norway they move in such hosts at times that a boat makes its way with difficulty through the compact mass. I do not speak at a venture; for I have received this incident from a scientific gentleman who witnessed it on the coast. This fish, less aristocratic than the Salmon, is a universal food; but here it would seem to be enough for all.

The *Halibut*, which is so often mentioned for its size and abundance, is less generally known than the others. It is common in the Fisheries of Norway, Iceland, and Greenland. In our country its reputation is local. Even at the seaport of Norfolk, in Virginia, it does not appear to have been known before 1843, when its arrival was announced as that of a distinguished stranger: "Our market yesterday morning was enriched with a delicacy from the northern waters, the Halibut—a strange fish in these parts, known only to epicures and naturalists." The larger fish are sometimes coarse and far from delicate, but they furnish a substantial meal, while the smaller Halibut is much liked.

The *Cod* is perhaps the most generally diffused and abundant of all, for it swims in all the waters of this coast from the Frozen ocean to the southern limit, and in some places it is in immense numbers. It is a popular fish, and when cured or salted is an excellent food in all parts of the world. Palatable, digestible, and nutritious, the Cod, as compared with other fish, is as beef compared with other meats, so that its incalculable multitudes seem to be according to a wise economy of nature. A female Cod is estimated to contain 3,400,000 eggs. Talk of multiplication a hundredfold. Here it is to infinity. Imagine these million eggs grown into fish, and then the process of reproduction repeated, and you have numbers which, like astronomical distances, are beyond human conception. But here the ravenous powers of other fish are more destructive than any efforts of the fisherman.

Behind all these is the *Whale*, whose corporal dimensions fitly represent the space which he occupies in the Fisheries of the world, hardly diminished by petroleum or gas. On this extended coast and in all these seas he is at home. Here is his retreat and play-ground. This is especially the case with the Right Whale, or, according to whalers, the "*right* whale to catch," with his bountiful supply of oil and bone, who is everywhere throughout this region, appearing at all points and swarming its waters. At times they are very large. Kotzebue reports them at Ounalaska of fabulous proportions, called by the natives Aliamak, and so long "that people engaged at the opposite end of the fish must halloo very loud to be able to understand each other." There is another whale known as the Bow-Head, which is so much about Kodiak that it is sometimes called the Kodiak whale. The valuable Sperm Whale, whose head and hunch are so productive in spermaceti, belongs to a milder sea, but he sometimes strays to the Aleutians. The Narwhal, with his two long tusks of ivory, out of which was made the famous throne of the early Danish kings, belongs to the Frozen ocean; but he, too, strays into the straits below. As no sea is now *mare clausum*, all these may be pursued by a ship under any flag, except directly on the coast and within its territorial limit. And yet it seems as if the possession of this coast as a commercial base must necessarily give to its people peculiar advantages in this pursuit. What is now done under difficulties will be done then with facilities, such at least as neighborhood supplied to the natives even with their small craft.

In our country the Whale Fishery has been a great and prosperous commerce, counted by millions. It has yielded very considerable gains, and sometimes large fortunes. The town of New Bedford, one of the most beautiful in the world, has been enriched by this Fishery, and yet you cannot fail to remark the impediments which the business has been compelled to overcome. The ship has been fitted on the Atlantic coast for a voyage of two or three years, and all the crew have entered into a partnership with regard to the oil. Traversing two oceans, separated by a stormy cape, it reaches its distant destination at last in these northern seas, and commences its tardy work, interrupted by occasional rest and opportunity to refit at the Sandwich islands. This now will be changed, as the ship sallies forth from friendly harbors near the game which is its mighty chase.

From the Whale Fishery I turn to another branch of inquiry. Undoubtedly there are infinite numbers of fish on this coast; but in order to determine whether they can constitute a permanent and profitable Fishery there are at least three different considerations which must not be disregarded. (1.) The existence of banks or soundings. (2.) Proper climatic conditions for catching and curing the fish. (3.) A market.

(1.) The *necessity of banks or soundings* is according to reason. Fish are not caught in the deep ocean. It is their nature to seek the bottom, where they are found in some way by the fisherman, armed with trawl, seine, or hook. As among the ancient Romans private luxury provided tanks and ponds for the preservation of fish, so nature provides banks, which are only *immense fish-preserves.* Soundings attest their existence in a margin along the coast; but it becomes important to know if they actually exist to much extent away from the coast. On this point our information is already considerable, if not decisive.

The sea and straits of Behring as far as the Frozen ocean have been surveyed by a Naval Expedition of the United States under Commander John Rogers. From one of his charts now before me it appears that, beginning at the Frozen ocean and descending through Behring straits and Behring sea, embracing Kotzebue sound, Norton bay, and Bristol bay, to the peninsula of Alaska, a distance of more than twelve degrees, there are constant uninterrupted soundings from twenty to fifty fathoms, thus presenting an immense extent proper in this respect for fishery. The famous Dogger bank, between England and Holland, teeming with Cod and constituting an inexhaustible fishing ground, has ninety fathoms of water. South of Alaska another chart shows soundings along the coast, with a considerable extent of bank in the neighborhood of the Shumagins and Kodiak, being precisely where all the evidence shows the existence of Cod. These banks, north and south of Alaska, taken together, according to the indications of the two charts, have an extent unsurpassed by any other in the world.

There is another illustration full of instruction. It is a map of the world, in the new work of Murray on Mammals, "showing approximately the one hundred fathom line of soundings," prepared from information furnished by the Hydrographic Department of the British Admiralty. Here are all the soundings of the world. At a glance you discern the remarkable line on the Pacific coast, beginning at 40° of latitude and widening constantly in a northwesterly direction; then with a gentle concave to the coast, stretching from Sitka to the Aleutians, with a wide margin; and then embracing and covering Behring straits to the Frozen ocean; the whole space, as indicated on the map, seeming like an immense unbroken sea meadow adjoining the land, and constituting plainly the largest extent of soundings in length and breadth known in the world, larger even than those of Newfoundland added to those of Great Britain. This map, which has been prepared by a scientific authority, simply in the interest of science, is an unimpeachable and disinterested witness.

Actual experience is better authority still. I learn that the people of California have already found Cod banks in these seas, and not deterred by distance have begun to gather a harvest. In 1865 no less than seventeen vessels left San Francisco for Cod Fishery on the Asiatic coast. This was a long voyage, requiring eighty days in going and returning. On the way better grounds were discovered among the Aleutians, with a better fish; and then again, other fishing grounds, better in every way, were discovered south of Alaska, in the neighborhood of the Shumagins, with an excellent harbor at hand. Here one vessel began its work on the 14th May, and notwithstanding stormy weather finished it on the 24th July, having taken fifty-two thousand fish. The largest catch in a single day was twenty-three hundred. The average weight of the fish dried was three pounds. Old fishermen compared the fish in taking and quality with that of Newfoundland. Large profits are anticipated. While fish from the Atlantic side bring at San Francisco not less than twelve cents a pound it is supposed that Shumagin fish at only eight cents a pound will yield a better return than the coasting trade. It remains to be seen if these flattering reports are confirmed by further experience.

From an opposite quarter is other confirmation. Here is a letter, which I have just received from Charles Bryant, Esq., at present a member of the Massachusetts Legislature, but for eighteen years acquainted with these seas, where he was engaged in the Whale Fishery. After mentioning the timber at certain places as a reason for the acquisition of these possessions, he says:

"But the chiefest value, and this alone is worth more than the pittance asked for it, consists in its extensive Cod and Halibut fish grounds. To the eastward of Kodiak or Aleutian islands are extensive banks or shoals nearly if not quite equal in extent to those of Newfoundland, and as well stocked with fish. Also west of the Aleutian islands, which extend from Alaska southwest half way to Kamtschatka, and inclosing that part of land laid down as Bristol bay, and west of it, is an extensive area of sea varying from forty fathoms in depth to twenty, where I have found the supply of codfish and halibut unfailing. These islands furnish good harbors for curing and preparing fish, as well as shelter in storm."

In another letter Mr. Bryant says that the shoals east of the entrance to Cook's inlet widen as they extend southward to latitude 50°; and that there are also large shoals south of Prince William sound, and again off Cross sound and Sitka. The retired ship-master adds that he never examined these shoals to ascertain their exact limits, but only incidentally, in the course of his regular business, that he might know when and where to obtain fish if he wished them. His report goes beyond any charts or soundings which I have seen, although the charts are coincident with it as far as they go. Cook particularly notices soundings in Bristol bay and in various places along the coast. Other navigators have done the same. Careful surveys have accomplished so much that at this time the bottom of Behring sea and of Behring straits as far as the Frozen ocean, constituting one immense bank, is completely known in its depth and character.

Add to all this the official report of Mr. Giddings, acting surveyor of Washington Territory, made to the Secretary of the Interior in 1866, where he says:

"Along the coast, between Cape Flattery and Sitka, in the Russian possessions, both Cod and Halibut are very plenty, and of a much larger size than those taken at the cape or further up the straits and sound. No one who knows these facts doubts that if vessels similar to those used by the bank fishermen from Massachusetts and Maine were fitted out here and were to fish on the *various banks along this coast* it would even now be a most lucrative business. The Cod and Halibut on this coast, up near Sitka, are fully equal to the largest taken in the eastern waters."

From all this evidence, including maps and personal experience, it is easy to see that the first condition of a considerable Fishery is not wanting.

(2.) *Proper climatic conditions* must exist also. The proverbial hardihood of fishermen has its limits. Elsewhere weather and storm have compelled the abandonment of banks which promised to be profitable. On a portion of this coast there can be no such rigors. South of Alaska and the Aleutians, and also in Bristol bay, immediately to the north of Alaska, the fishing grounds will compare in temperature with those of Newfoundland or Norway. It is more important to know if the fish when taken can be properly cured. This is one of the privileges of northern skies. Within the tropics fish may be taken in abundance, but the constant sun does not allow their preservation. The constant rains of Sitka, with only a few bright days in the year, must prevent the work of curing on any considerable scale. But the navigators make frequent mention of dry or preserved fish on the coast, and it is understood that fish are now cured at

Kodiak. It had for a long time been customary on this island to dry seal flesh in the air, which could not be done on the main land. Thus the opportunity of curing the fish seems to exist near the very banks where they are taken. But the California fishermen carry their fish home to be cured, in which they imitate the fishermen of Gloucester. As the yearly fishing product of this port is larger than that of any other in North America, perhaps in the world, this example cannot be without weight.

(3.) The *market* also is of prime necessity. Fish are not caught and cured except for a market. Besides the extended coast, where an immediate demand must always prevail in proportion to an increasing population, there is an existing market in California, which is attested by long voyages to Kamtschatka for fish and by recent attempts to find fishing grounds. San Francisco at one time took from Okhotsk nine hundred tons of fish, being about one eighth of the yearly fishing product of Gloucester. Her fishing vessels last year brought home from the Shumagin banks fifteen hundred tons of dried fish and ten thousand gallons of cod liver oil. There is also a growing market in Washington and Oregon, too, unless I am misinformed. But beyond the domestic market, spreading from the coast into the interior, there will be a foreign market of no limited amount. Mexico, Central America, and the States of South America, all Catholic in religion, will require this subsistence, and being southern in climate they must look northward for a supply. The two best customers of our Atlantic fisheries are Hayti and Cuba, two Catholic countries under a southern sun. The fishermen of Massachusetts began at an early day to send their Cod to Portugal, Spain, and Italy, all Catholic countries under a southern sun. Our "salt" fish became popular. The Portugese minister at London in 1784, in a conference with Mr. Adams on a commercial treaty with the United States, mentioned "salt fish" among the objects most needed in his country, and added, "the consumption of this article in Portugal is immense, and he would avow, that the American salt fish was preferred to any other on account of its quality." (John Adams's Writings, vol. 8, p. 339.) Such facts are more than curious.

But more important than the Pacific States of the American continent are the great empires of Japan and China, with uncounted populations depending much on fish. In China one tenth subsist on fish. Notwithstanding the considerable supplies at home, it does not seem impossible for an energetic and commercial people to find a market here of inconceivable magnitude, which will dwarf that original fur trade with China that was once so tempting.

From this survey you can all judge this question of the Fisheries, which I only state without assuming to determine. You can judge if well-stocked fishing banks have been found under such conditions of climate and market as to supply a new and important Fishery. Already the people of California have anticipated the answer, and their enterprise has arrested attention in Europe. The Journal of Peterman, The *Geographische Mittheilungen*, for the present year, which is the authentic German record of geographical science, borrows from a San Francisco paper to announce these successful voyages as the beginning of a new commerce. If this be so, as there is reason to believe, these coasts and seas will have a new value. The future only can disclose the form they may take. They may be a Newfoundland, a Norway, a Scotland, or perhaps a New England, with another Gloucester and another New Bedford.

Influence of Fisheries.

An eminent French writer, an enthusiast on fishes, Lacepéde, has depicted the influence of Fisheries, which he illustrates by the herring, calling it "one of those natural products whose use has decided the destiny of nations." Without adopting these strong words it is easy to see that such Fisheries as seem about to be opened on the Pacific must exercise a wonderful influence over the population there, while they give a new spring to commerce and enlarge the national resources. In these aspects it is impossible to exaggerate. Fishermen are not as other men. They have a character of their own, taking its complexion from their life. In ancient Rome they had a peculiar holiday with games, known as *Piscatorii Ludi*. The first among us in this pursuit were the Pilgrims, who even before they left Leyden looked to fishing for a support in their new home, on which King James remarked: "So God have my soul, 'tis an honest trade; 'twas the apostles' own calling." As soon as they reached Plymouth they began to fish, and not long afterwards appropriated the profits of the Fisheries at Cape Cod to found a free school. From this Puritan origin are derived those Fisheries which for a while were our chief commerce, and still continue an important element of national wealth. The Cod Fisheries of the United States are now valued at more than two million dollars annually. Even they are inferior to the French Fisheries, whose annual product is more than three million dollars; and these again are small by the side of the British Fisheries, whose annual product is not far from twenty-five million dollars. Such an interest must be felt far and near, commercially and financially, while it contributes to the comfort of all. How soon it may prevail on the Pacific who can say? But this Treaty is the beginning.

Of course it is difficult to estimate what is so uncertain, or at least is prospective only. Our own Fisheries, now so considerable, were small in the beginning; they were small even when they inspired the eloquence of Burke in that most splendid page never equaled even by himself. But the Continental Congress, in its original instructions to its commissioners for the negotiation of peace with Great Britain, required as a fundamental condition, next to Independence, that these Fisheries should be preserved unimpaired. While this proposition was under discussion Elbridge Gerry, who had grown up among the fishermen of Massachusetts, repelled the attacks upon their pursuit in words which are not out of place here. "It is not so much fishing," he said, "as enterprise, industry, employment. It is not so much fish; it is gold, the produce of that avocation. It is the employment of those who would otherwise be idle, the food of those who would otherwise be hungry, the wealth of those who would otherwise be poor." After debate it was resolved by Congress that "the common right of taking fish should in no case be given up." For this principle the eldest Adams contended with ability and constancy until it was fixed in the treaty, where it stands side by side with the acknowledgment of Independence.

In the discussions which ended thus triumphantly the argument for the Fisheries was stated most compactly by Ralph Izard, of South Carolina, in a letter to John Adams, dated at Paris, 24th September, 1778; and what he said then may be repeated now:

"Since the advantages of commerce have been well understood, the fisheries have been looked upon by the naval Powers of Europe as an object of the greatest importance. The French have been increasing their fishery ever since the treaty of Utrecht, which has enabled them to rival Great Britain at sea. The fisheries of Holland were not only the first rise of the Republic, but have been the constant support of all her commerce and navigation. This branch of trade is of such concern to the Dutch that in their public prayers they are said to request the Supreme Being that it would please Him to bless the Government, the lords, the States, and also the fisheries. The fishery of Newfoundland appears to me to be a mine of infinitely greater value than Mexico and Peru. It enriches the proprietors, is worked at less expense, and is the source of naval strength and protection."—*John Adams's Works*, vol. 7, p. 45.

I have grouped these allusions that you may see how the Fisheries of that day, though comparatively small, enlisted the energies of our fathers. Tradition confirms this record. The sculptured image of a Cod hanging from the ceiling in the hall of the Massachusetts House of Representatives, where it was placed during the last century, constantly recalls this industrial and commercial staple with the great part which it performed. And now it is my duty to remind you that these Fisheries, guarded so watchfully and vindicated with such conquering zeal, had a value prospective rather than present, or at least small compared with what it is now. Exact figures, covering the ten years between 1765 and 1775, show that during this period Massachusetts employed annually in the Fisheries 665 vessels amounting to 25,620 tons, and only 4,405 men. In contrast with this interest, which seems so small, although at the time considerable, are the present Fisheries of our country; and here again we have exact figures. The number of vessels in the Cod Fishery alone in 1861, just before the blight of the war reached this business, was 2,753 amounting to 137,665 tons, and with 19,271 men, being more than four times as many vessels and men, and more than five times as much tonnage, as for ten years preceding the Revolution was employed annually by Massachusetts, representing at that time the fishing interest of the country.

Small beginnings, therefore, are no discouragement to me, and I turn with confidence to the future. Already the local Fisheries on this coast have developed among the generations of natives a singular gift in building and managing their small craft so as to excite the frequent admiration of voyagers. The larger Fisheries there will naturally exercise a corresponding influence on the population destined to build and manage the larger craft. The beautiful baidar will give way to the fishing-smack, the clipper, and the steamer. All things will be changed in form and proportion; but the original aptitude for the sea will remain. A practical race of intrepid navigators will swarm the coast, ready for any enterprise of business or patriotism. Commerce will find new arms; the country new defenders; the national flag new hands to bear it aloft.

SUMMARY.

Mr. President, I now conclude this examination. From a review of the origin of the Treaty, and the general considerations with regard to it we have passed to an examination of these possessions under different heads, in order to arrive at a knowledge of their character and value; and here we have noticed the existing Government, which was found to be nothing but a fur company, whose only object is trade; then the Population, where a very few Russians and Creoles are a scanty fringe to the aboriginal races; then the Climate, a ruling influence, with its thermal current of ocean and its eccentric isothermal line, by which the rigors of that coast are tempered to a mildness unknown in the same latitude on the Atlantic side; then, the Vegetable Products, so far as known, chief among which are forests of pine and fir waiting for the ax; then the Mineral Products, among which are coal and copper, if not iron, silver, lead, and gold, besides the two great products of New England, "granite and ice;" then the Furs, including precious skins of the Black Fox and Sea Otter, which originally tempted the settlement, and have remained to this day the exclusive object of pursuit; and lastly, the Fisheries, which, in waters superabundant with animal life beyond any of the globe, seem to promise a new commerce to the country. All these I have presented plainly and impartially, exhibiting my authorities as I proceeded. I have done little more than hold the scales. If these have inclined on either side it is because reason or testimony on that side was the weightier.

WHAT REMAINS TO BE DONE.

As these extensive possessions, constituting a corner of the continent, pass from the imperial Government of Russia they will naturally receive a new name. They will be no longer Russian America. How shall they be called? Clearly any name borrowed from classical history or from individual invention will be little better than a misnomer or a nickname unworthy of such an occasion. Even if taken from our own history it will be of doubtful taste. The name should come from the country itself. It should be indigenous, aboriginal, one of the autochthons of the soil. Happily such a name exists, which is as proper in sound as in origin. It appears from the report of Cook, the illustrious navigator, to whom I have so often referred, that the euphonious name now applied to the peninsula which is the continental link of the Aleutian chain was the sole word used originally by the native islanders "when speaking of the American continent in general, which they knew perfectly well to be a great land." It only remains that, following these natives, whose places are now ours, we, too, should call this "great land" Alaska.

Another change must be made without delay. As the settlements of this coast came *Eastward* from Russia, bringing with them the Russian flag Western time, the day is earlier by twenty-four hours with them than with us; so that their Sunday is our Saturday, and the other days of the week are in corresponding discord. This must be rectified according to the national meridian, so that there shall be the same Sunday for all, and the other days of the week shall be in corresponding harmony. Important changes must follow, of which this is typical. All else must be rectified according to the national meridian, so that within the sphere of our common country there shall be everywhere the same generous rule and one prevailing harmony. Of course, the unreformed Julian calendar, received from Russia, will give place to ours; Old Style yielding to New Style.

An object of immediate practical interest will be the survey of the extended and indented coast by our own officers, bringing it all within the domain of science and assuring to navigation much-needed assistance, while the Republic is honored by a continuation of national charts, where execution vies with science, and the art of engraving is the beautiful handmaid. Associated with this survey, and scarcely inferior in value, will be the examination of the country by scientific explorers, so that its geological structure may become known with its various products, vegetable and mineral. But your best work and most important endowment will be the Republican Government, which, looking to a long future, you will organize, with schools free to all and with equal laws, before which every citizen will stand erect in the consciousness of manhood. Here will be a motive power, without which Coal itself will be insufficient. Here will be a source of wealth more inexhaustible than any Fisheries. Bestow such a government, and you will bestow what is better than all you can receive, whether quintals of fish, sands of gold, choicest fur, or most beautiful ivory.

www.ingramcontent.com/pod-product-compliance
Lightning Source LLC
Chambersburg PA
CBHW032122080426
42733CB00008B/1015